HE FREEDOM IN CHRIST MESSAGE FOR THE MILLENNIAL GENERATION

UP

D

disciple

LIFE • FREEDOM • PURPOSE

Published by Monarch Books

an imprint of

Lion Hudson plc

Wilkinson House, Jordan Hill Road,

Oxford OX2 8DR, England

Email: monarch@lionhudson.com

www.lionhudson.com/monarch

ISBN: 978-0-85721-698-4

E-ISBN: 978-0-85721-699-1

First edition 2016

A catalogue record for this book is available from the British Library

Printed and bound in the UK, March 2016, LH26

Acknowledgments

Credits and thanks

Our grateful thanks go to Dr. Neil T. Anderson, the Founder of Freedom In Christ Ministries, whose amazing teaching inspired *disciple*, and to the 69 individuals who made donations to enable this project to get off the ground. Without you, *disciple* would never have happened. Thanks too to the amazing team who worked on the project:

Producer: Steve Goss

Writers: Steve Goss, Jess Regnart, Dan Lodge, David Edwards, Rob Peabody, André Adefope

Design concepts: Jon Smethurst

Coffee Shop Films:

Presenters: David Edwards, Rob Peabody, Jess Regnart, André Adefope

Logistics: Rob Davies, Zoë Goss

Production (UCB Broadcast):

Andrew Walkington, Executive Producer

Ben Emery, Director

Malcolm Salt, Production Manager

Mark Tennant, Audio Engineer

Morgan Griffith, Audio Engineer

Luke Campbell, Camera Operator

Naomi Chandler, Camera Operator

Becky Welford, Camera Operator

Set design and dressing: Benn Price, Ben Poole, Sam Frawley, Amy Meadham

Set building: Roy Emery, Hugh Graham, Mark Kirshaw, Ryan Downes

Starter Films:

Presenter: Dan Lodge

Director: Rick Holland (Blink Media)

US Testimony Filming:

Co-ordinator: Trenidy Davis

Production of the written material:

Editor: Jenny Ward

Layout: Steve Goss

App design:

All round genius: Daniel Upton

Picture Credits

p.38 FreeImages.com/s s

p.49 FreeImages.com/Martin BOULANGER

p.55 FreeImages.com/Rene Asmussenfoto

p.81 FreeImages.com/Yazıcı Ekrem

p.85 FreeImages.com/Alexander Popelier

p.98 FreeImages.com/John Evans

p.109 FreeImages.com/Steve Knight

p.140 FreeImages.com/John Nyberg

p.153 FreeImages.com/Mike Bamford

p.154 FreeImages.com/Einar Hansen

p.165 FreeImages.com/Vicky Johnson

Contents

LEADER'S GUIDE

Welcome to *disciple*!

disciple has been born out of a deep passion to see young adults connecting with Jesus and making a radical difference with their lives. Our prayer is that it will be a highly effective tool in your hands.

Freedom In Christ Ministries exists to help Christian leaders make fruitful disciples. Please register with us (see below) and, if we can help you in any way as you run the course, do get in touch.

For your convenience, we have divided this Leader's Guide into two sections. So that you do not also have to have a Participant's Guide, we have duplicated the Participant's Guide on pages 7 to 192. These pages are exactly the same as the book that participants have (with the same page numbers).

The second section contains notes specifically for course leaders and starts on page 193. You will find it very helpful to read "Understanding *disciple*" and "Leading *disciple*" before you begin.

Have fun as you help people take hold of these life-changing truths!

Please Register

It costs nothing and you will get:

- **access to a special section of the Freedom In Christ website with downloads that you will find useful when running your course.**
- **details of training available in your area.**
- **occasional news from Freedom In Christ (optional).**

Register at www.ficm.org.uk/register

Connect with us

The *disciple* app contains a heap of helpful additional input as you progress through *disciple:*

- **Six extra teaching films with Rob, Jess, and David**
- **Truth Encounter lists at your fingertips**
- **Create your own "Stronghold-Buster" and get daily reminders to use it**
- **Watch the Starter Film before each session.**

Search for "disciple – Freedom In Christ" in your app store.

Join the *disciple* Facebook group

- Share your thoughts, questions, and stories
- Keep up to date with the world of Freedom In Christ
- From Facebook, search for "disciple", select the "closed group", and ask to join.

Find your local Freedom In Christ website

We operate in around 40 countries. Find your nearest office or representative at www.ficminternational.org.

- Our US site is at: www.ficm.org
- Our UK site is at: www.ficm.org.uk

Register on our UK site to receive our daily devotional by email.

Meet the team

DAVID EDWARDS was born on the sunny island of Trinidad in the Caribbean where he spent most of his formative years. He moved to the UK as a teenager and started a career in health and social care management. In 2010 David answered his call to full time pastoral ministry and resigned from his career. He currently pastors a congregation in Cheshire, England, where he lives with his wife, Linda, and their foster son Joshua. He is also the University Chaplain of Manchester Metropolitan University, where he gives pastoral support to both staff and students. David loves singing and was once runner-up in the London "Soloist of the Year" competition.

JESS REGNART works for Freedom In Christ Ministries equipping church leaders to disciple teenagers and young adults. Having grown up in an atheist/agnostic household she knows first-hand how hard it is to live without knowing God. After something of a Damascus road conversion in her early twenties she fell head over heels for Jesus and went on to complete a theology degree. Jess has a huge passion to help teenagers and young adults meet Jesus and see Him for who He really is. She also has a large shoe collection, loves Miss Piggy, hates bananas, and is learning to longboard with her dog.

ROB PEABODY serves as the Cofounder and International Director of Awaken, a non-profit organization that exists to resource the Church for action. In 2011, Rob, along with his wife, Medea, and their two boys, left his position as lead campus pastor of a megachurch in Texas, USA, to pioneer fresh expressions of church seeking to engage unreached 20s and 30s in northeast London, UK. He leads the International Mission Board, and heads up Fresh Expressions' pioneering efforts amongst the next generation. Rob has written multiple books and film resources (more info at awakenmovement.com). Rob is a fanatic about cinnamon ice cream, once got escorted by state troopers out of the Texas Governor's office after hours, cycled from London to Paris in 2013, and is definitely not a morning person.

DAN LODGE works as part of the resources team for Youth for Christ. His passion is to see churches equip young people to be able to go and share their faith. His role sees him creating resources for 11–25s as well as travelling and speaking all over the place. He has a hatred of tomatoes and loves nothing more than being spoken about in the third person.

ANDRÉ ADEFOPE (who features in the extra film on *The Gift Of Sex*) became a Christian at a talk entitled "sex before marriage" having previously struggled with self-image issues, being let down by friends, and romantic disasters. He has a keen interest in helping people apply God's Word to the area of dating and singleness. He is Head of Relationship Development at Visible Ministries in Manchester, UK, and oversees the "Relationship Dilemma" project. He is also an undefeated table tennis champion (though only in the Visible office).

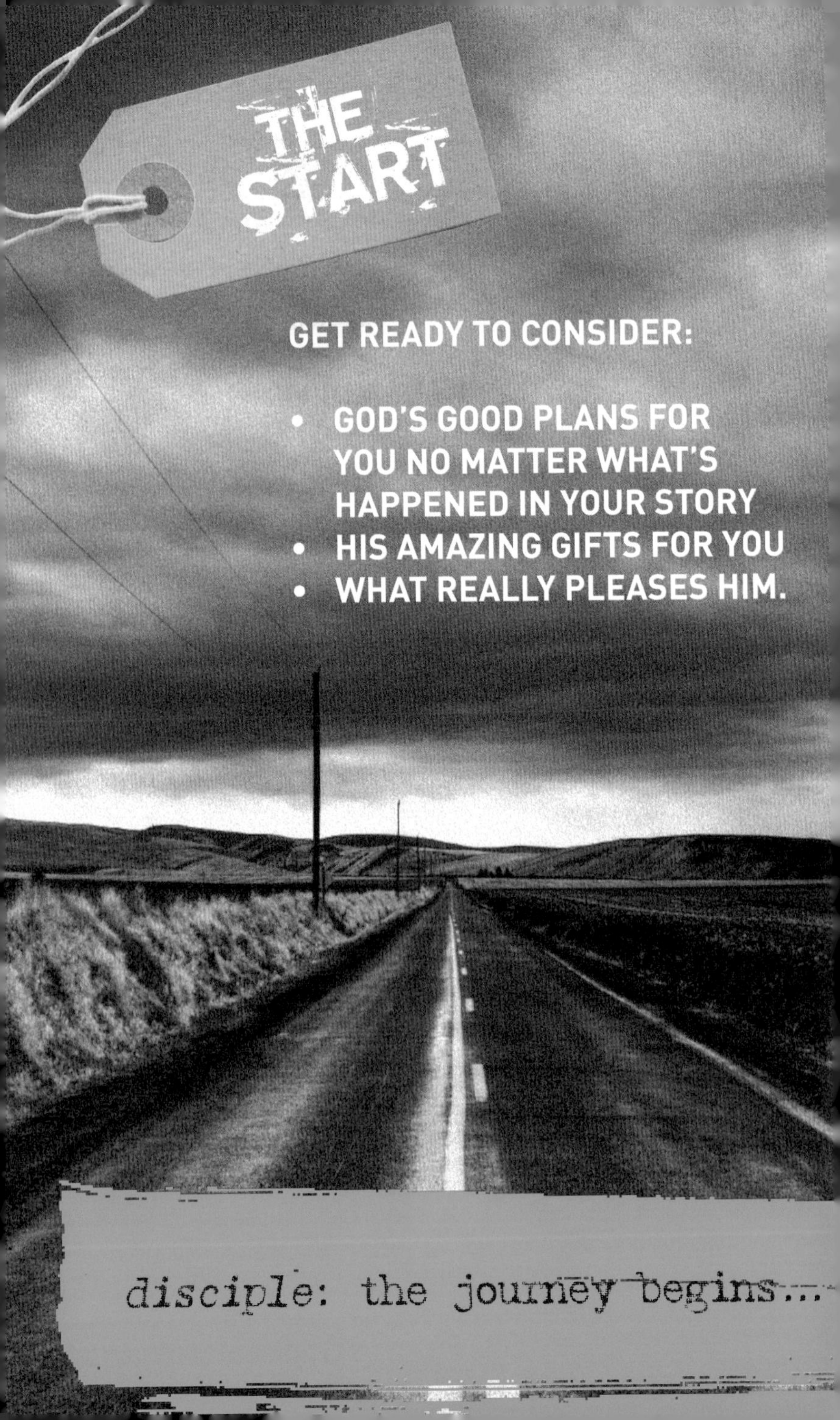
THE START
GET READY TO CONSIDER:
• GOD'S GOOD PLANS FOR YOU NO MATTER WHAT'S HAPPENED IN YOUR STORY
• HIS AMAZING GIFTS FOR YOU
• WHAT REALLY PLEASES HIM.
disciple: the journey begins...

01

Your unwritten autobiography

For we are God's handiwork, created in Christ Jesus to do good works, which God prepared in advance for us to do.

Ephesians 2:10

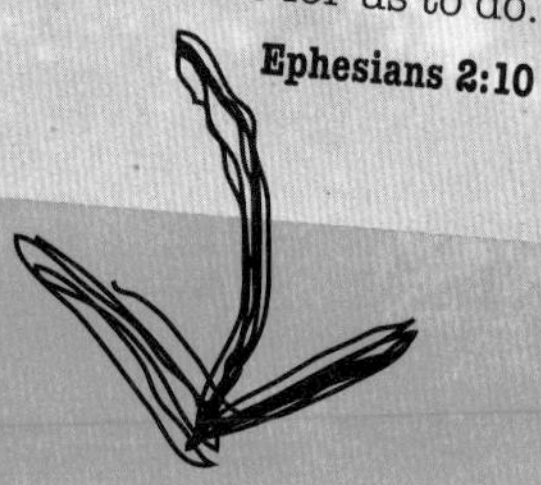

If you are a Christian, you already have everything you need for your life story to make an impact that will last for ever.

What story are you going to write?

When you were young, what did you want to be when you grew up?

How realistic do you think it is to imagine that your life from this point on could make a genuinely positive impact in the world?

1

Outrageous plans:

"For I know the plans I have for you," declares the Lord, "plans to prosper you and not to harm you, plans to give you hope and a future."

Jeremiah 29:11

God has a superb, outrageously amazing plan for your life which he planned for you before you were even born.

According to sociologists our generation is more self-obsessed than any generation that has come before.

Even when you get all the material and worldly things you think you want – there is still a void, a sense of pointlessness.

Narcissism:
inordinate fascination with oneself; excessive self-love; vanity. Synonyms: self-centeredness, smugness, egocentrism. (dictionary.com)

Chat

Thinking about what you wanted to be when you grew when you were a child, did this change over the years? If so, why did it change?

Looking to the future, if you were to list three things you want from the rest of your life, what would they be?

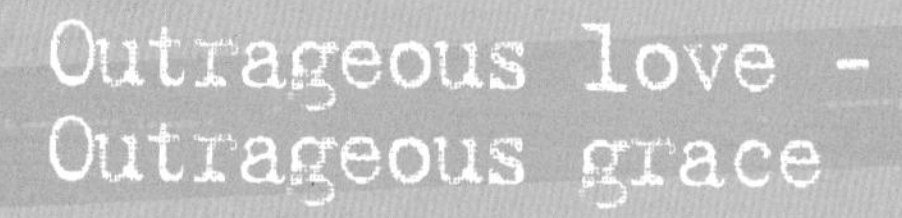

2 Outrageous love - Outrageous grace

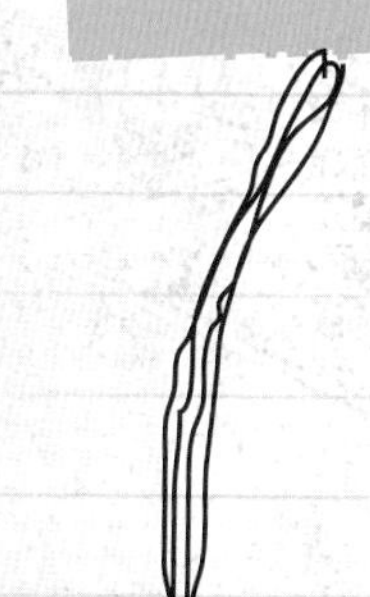

- You already have everything you need to make your life count for eternity and fulfil the plans God has for you – if you have become a child of God.
- God likes, delights, and loves you unconditionally no matter what you have done or might do in the future.
- No one has a back story too bad or messed up to become the person God created them to be and make their life count!

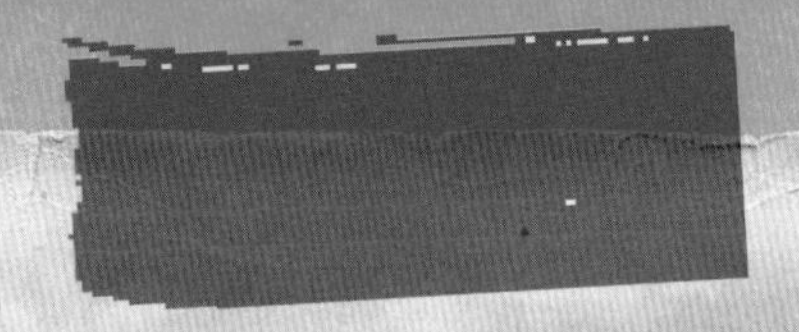

The Parable of the Lost Son

Jesus continued: "There was a man who had two sons. The younger one said to his father, 'Father, give me my share of the estate.' So he divided his property between them. "Not long after that, the younger son got together all he had, set off for a distant country and there squandered his wealth in wild living. After he had spent everything, there was a severe famine in that whole country, and he began to be in need. So he went and hired himself out to a citizen of that country, who sent him to his fields to feed pigs. He longed to fill his stomach with the pods that the pigs were eating, but no one gave him anything.

"When he came to his senses, he said, 'How many of my father's hired men have food to spare, and here I am starving to death! I will set out and go back to my father and say to him: Father, I have sinned against heaven and against you. I am no longer worthy to be called your son; make me like one of your hired men.' So he got up and went to his father.

"But while he was still a long way off, his father saw him and was filled with compassion for him; he ran to his son, threw his arms around him and kissed him. The son said to him, 'Father, I have sinned against heaven and against you. I am no longer worthy to be called your son.' But the father said to his servants, 'Quick! Bring the best robe and put it on him. Put a ring on his finger and sandals on his feet. Bring the fattened calf and kill it. Let's have a feast and celebrate. For this son of mine was dead and is alive again; he was lost and is found.' So they began to celebrate."

Luke 15:11–24

Like the younger son, we have been given: the robe – we have been restored to a position of "right standing" with God; the ring – we have incredible power and authority in Christ; and the sandals – we have become children of God Himself and have all the rights and privileges of children.

Can you identify yourself with the younger son in the story? If so, in what ways?

How does the father in the story change the way you think about God and your relationship with Him?

Which of the items given to the younger son (and therefore to you too) is most significant to you? Why? What difference will knowing this make to you day to day?

EXTRA FILM ON THE APP

WHY BELIEVE THE BIBLE?

Outrageous choice

The older brother thought he could please his father by working hard and doing the right thing. He was angry when the father simply accepted his little brother back and didn't even punish him. He didn't realize that he was already pleasing to his father just because of who he was.

The point Jesus was making is that God does not love you because of the good things you do. Or stop loving you when you do terrible things. In fact it's not about what you do at all. He loves you for who you are.

Disciple:
someone who is learning to become more and more like Jesus in character, and who will therefore behave more and more like Him.

Reflect

At the end of every session, we encourage you to have a time of reflection. Consider questions such as the following: What has God shown you today? What points have particularly struck you? Have you become aware of any faulty thinking, anything you have believed that you now realize is not in line with what is actually true according to God? If so, write it down on the pages at the end of this book.

Making our life stories count is not about trying harder or striving to follow God. It's simply about knowing God and knowing who you are. It all flows from your God-given identity and relationship with Jesus. However, it's by no means inevitable that you'll leave an eternal legacy – and making the choice to do so goes right against the prevailing culture.

There are things that want to hold you back and will do if you let them. But *disciple* will help you work out what they are and how to overcome them – every time.

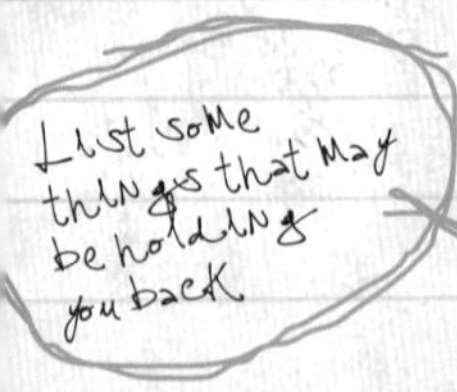

Going deeper

In the "Going deeper" section, you will find suggestions for things you can work on at home in between sessions in order to take the truths deeper. The *disciple* app has some additional help on that.

The truths in this session can be absolutely life changing if you can really take hold of them in your heart.

- Read through Luke 15:11–24 (it's printed on page 18) and then take some time in quiet prayer to imagine the story again. Imagine yourself as the son or daughter returning, and God as the father. How does it make you feel to know that once you return to Him, you are loved completely and unconditionally, no matter what has happened to you or what you have done in your life?

- Think again about the ring, the robe, and the sandals and what they symbolize. Remind yourself that, if you're a Christian, you <u>already</u> have them. Spend some time with God making a choice to use them in your life.

- Read the rest of the story (Luke 15:25–32). Can you recognize anything of the older brother's attitude in you? In your relationship with God are you more like a son or a servant?

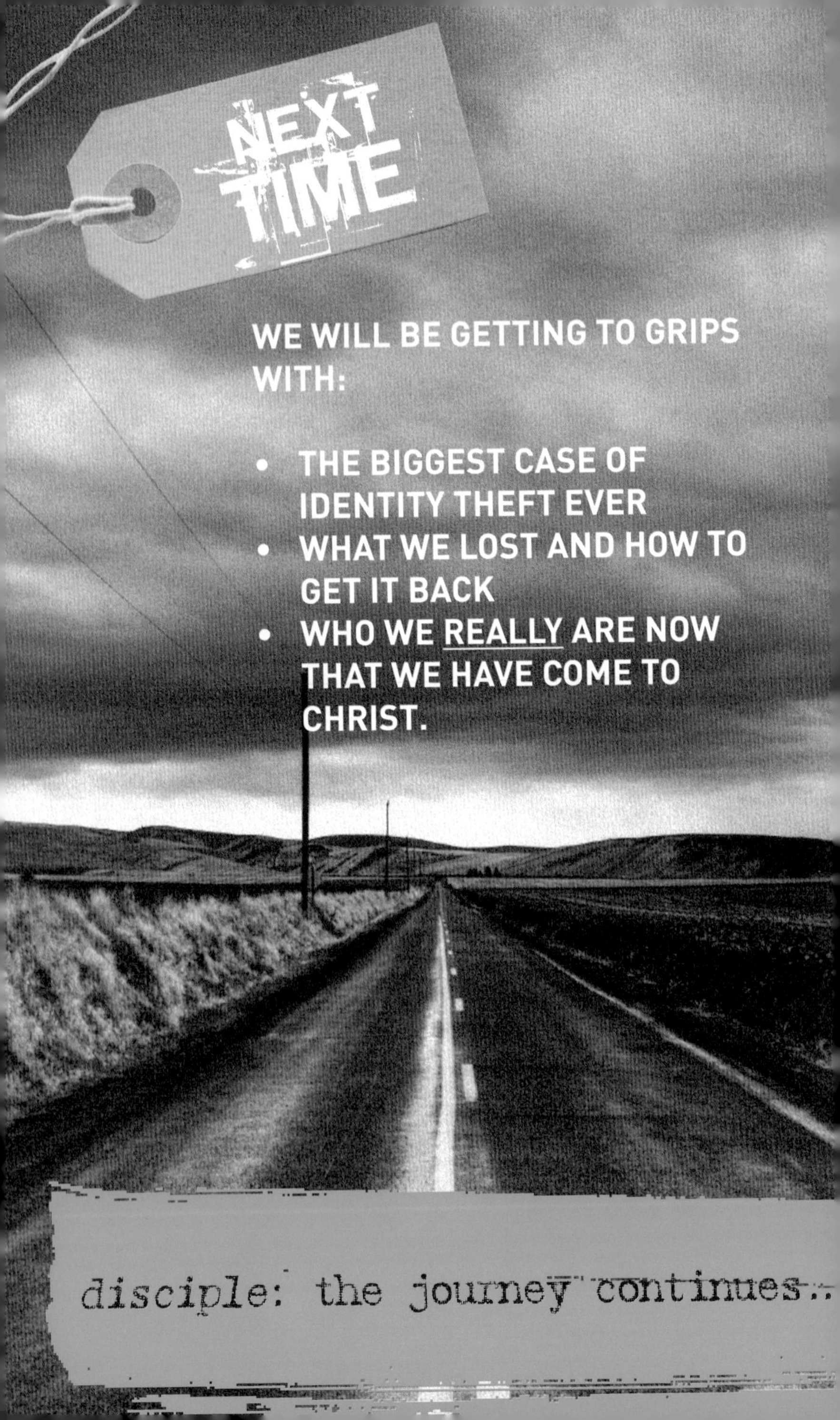
NEXT TIME
WE WILL BE GETTING TO GRIPS WITH:
• THE BIGGEST CASE OF IDENTITY THEFT EVER
• WHAT WE LOST AND HOW TO GET IT BACK
• WHO WE REALLY ARE NOW THAT WE HAVE COME TO CHRIST.
disciple: the journey continues...

02

How the story starts

WHY?

Paul, an apostle of Christ Jesus by the will of God;
To God's holy people in Ephesus, the faithful in Christ Jesus.

Ephesians 1:1

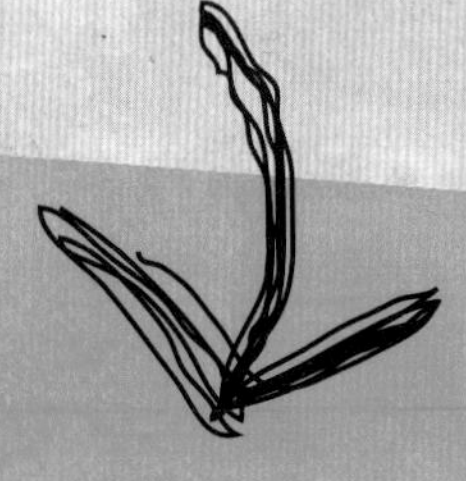

The disobedience of Adam and Eve left us spiritually dead with driving needs to be significant, secure, and accepted. Becoming Christians meant a huge change in our identity and story. We are no longer spiritual orphans but holy people who are spiritually alive! And all our needs are now met in Christ.

If you were introduced to someone you didn't know, what is the most surprising thing you could tell them about yourself, something you did, or something that happened to you?

What are some of the key things that give you a sense of your own unique identity? (They may perhaps be to do with your culture, your achievements, your role in life, or other things).

The problem:

So God created mankind in his own image, in the image of God he created them; male and female he created them.

Genesis 1:27

As for you, you were dead in your transgressions and sins.

Ephesians 2:1

We are more than we see – we are made in God's image which means that we are spiritual beings too.

At the fall Adam and Eve messed things up for us. It was a total catastrophe for humankind.

We are all now born spiritually dead with a driving need to find the significance, security, and acceptance that they lost.

What (if anything) do you know about your ancestors and your family tree?

Can you see ways of thinking and acting that have been passed down your family line? For example are there things that your ancestors were good at that you are too, or things that they struggled with that you do too?

How different do you think life would be if we had not been born spiritually dead but instead were born connected to God and were able to chat with Him as we are chatting to one another now?

2

The cure

- If you are a Christian you are now part of God's story and restored as His child.

- When we came to Christ we were reconnected to God and our spiritual life was restored.

- All Christians have become a brand new creation. We are holy ones (saints) – no matter what our back story is!

- The significance, security, and acceptance we were designed to have are fully restored to us in Jesus.

Astonishing truths about who you now are!

Yet to all who did receive him, to those who believed in his name, he gave the right to become children of God.

John 1:12

"I have come that they may have life, and have it to the full."

John 10:10

"Whoever has the Son has LIFE. Whoever does not have the Son of God does not have LIFE."

1 John 5:12

"I am the resurrection and the LIFE. He who believes in me will LIVE, even though they die."

John 11:25

Therefore, if anyone is in Christ, he is a new creation. The old has passed away; behold, the new has come.

2 Corinthians 5:17 (ESV)

God made him who had no sin to be sin for us, so that in him we might become the righteousness of God.

2 Corinthians 5:21

Chat

How hard do you find it to believe that, since you are in Christ, you have become a holy one, a saint, without any effort on your part? Why?

What difference would it make to your life to know that, deep down, you are a delight to God just because of who you now are and that nothing and nobody can change that?

Will knowing this be more likely to make you think, "So I can live however I like" or "I really want to serve God, not because I have to but because I want to"? Why?

3

Great news!

Whoever does not love does not know God, because God is love.

1 John 4:8

Therefore, there is now no condemnation for those who are in Christ Jesus.

Romans 8:1

My dear children, I write this to you so that you will not sin. But if anybody does sin, we have an advocate with the Father—Jesus Christ, the Righteous One.

1 John 2:1

God loves us no matter what we have done or what we do.

We may not feel significant, secure, and accepted but we need to start with what God says is true, not our feelings. What you believe about yourself will always work out in how you behave.

We do still go wrong. But when that happens, it doesn't change the fact that we are holy ones. We simply need to acknowledge our mistake, say sorry, and choose not to do it again.

Who we are

What we do

Who I Am In Jesus

I renounce the lie that I am rejected, unloved, dirty, or shameful because in Jesus I am completely ACCEPTED. God says that:

I am God's child (see John 1:12)

I am Jesus' friend (see John 15:15)

I have been justified (see Romans 5:1)

I am united with God and I am one spirit with Him (see 1 Corinthians 6:17)

I have been bought with a price: I belong to God (see 1 Corinthians 6:19–20)

I am a member of Jesus' body (see 1 Corinthians 12:27)

I am a saint, a holy one (see Ephesians 1:1)

I have been adopted as God's child (see Ephesians 1:5)

I have direct access to God through the Holy Spirit (see Ephesians 2:18)

I am forgiven of all my sins (see Colossians 1:14)

I am complete in Jesus (see Colossians 2:10)

I renounce the lie that I am guilty, unprotected, alone, or abandoned because in Jesus I am totally SECURE. God says that:

I am free forever from condemnation (see Romans 8:1–2)

I am assured that all things work together for good (see Romans 8:28)

I am free from all condemning charges against me (see Romans 8:31–34)

I cannot be separated from the love of God (see Romans 8:35–39)

I have been established, anointed, and sealed by God (see 2 Corinthians 1:21–22)

I am confident that the good work God has begun in me will be perfected (see Philippians 1:6)

I am a citizen of heaven (see Philippians 3:20)

I am hidden with Jesus in God (see Colossians 3:3)

I have not been given a spirit of fear, but of power, love, and a sound mind (see 2 Timothy 1:7)

I can find grace and mercy to help me when I need it (see Hebrews 4:16)

I am born of God and the evil one cannot touch me (see 1 John 5:18)

I renounce the lie that I am worthless, inadequate, helpless, or hopeless because in Jesus I am deeply SIGNIFICANT. God says that:

I am the salt of the earth and the light of the world (see Matthew 5:13–14)

I am a branch of the true vine, Jesus, a channel of His life (see John 15:1–5)

I have been chosen and appointed by God to bear fruit (see John 15:16)

I am a personal, Spirit empowered witness of Jesus (see Acts 1:8)

I am a temple of God (see 1 Corinthians 3:16)

I am a minister of reconciliation for God (see 2 Corinthians 5:17–21)

I am God's fellow worker (see 2 Corinthians 6:1)

I am seated with Jesus in the heavenly realms (see Ephesians 2:6)

I am God's workmanship, created for good works (see Ephesians 2:10)

I can come to God with freedom and confidence (see Ephesians 3:12)

I can do all things through Jesus who strengthens me (see Philippians 4:13)

I am not the great "I Am", but by the grace of God I am what I am (see Exodus 3:14; John 8:24, 28, 58; 1 Corinthians 15:10).

Reflect

Read through the "Who I Am In Jesus" list again.

Even better, get into twos and read the list slowly to your partner changing "I" to "you". So you would start by saying, "You are not rejected, unloved, dirty..." etc. and then "You are God's child" etc. Swap over when you have finished.

- Which truths stand out to you the most? Write them down or highlight them in your Bible.
- How does it make you feel to realize that Jesus paid with His life so that you could be reconnected to God and have an intimate relationship with him? Spend some time thanking God and telling Him how you feel.

When you realize that an area in your belief system is not in line with what God says is true, remember to write it down on pages 190–191 together with the corresponding truth.

Going deeper

In order to make sure you really get hold of these life-changing truths, find some time in the coming week to reflect on the following:

- Slowly read the "Who I Am In Jesus" list from this session out loud. Let each one sink in before moving on to the next one.
- Look up the Bible references alongside the items in the list.
- Do you accept that, if God says the things on the list are true of you, then they are true, no matter how you may feel?
- If you are struggling with this, why not take some quiet time with God and ask Him to show you how He sees you.

We recommend you continue to read the list out loud once or twice a day until you feel you have taken hold of who you really are in Jesus. It may take several weeks. You will find the list on the *disciple* app so why not use it whenever you have a spare moment?

NEXT TIME
WE WILL BE WORKING OUT:
• WHAT TRUTH IS AND WHETHER OR NOT IT IS TRUE FOR EVERYONE
• WHAT FAITH IS
• HOW WE CAN INCREASE OUR FAITH.
disciple: the journey continues.

03

A true story

Jesus answered, "You say that I am a king. In fact, the reason I was born and came into the world is to testify to the truth. Everyone on the side of truth listens to me."
"What is truth?" retorted Pilate.

John 18:37–38

"What is truth?" is a question that people have been asking for thousands of years.

Jesus didn't claim to know truth. He claimed actually to BE the truth.

Faith is simply making a choice to believe in Jesus as the truth rather than following feelings.

If you saw someone about to jump off a high wall because they had a sincerely-held belief that gravity wouldn't affect them, would you be prepared to disregard their belief and try to prevent them jumping? Or do you think there is a strong case for respecting their belief and not interfering? Why?

Tell the group about a time when you acted on false information, when you believed something that turned out not to be true.

Truth is true

"I am the way, and the truth, and the life; no one comes to the Father but through Me."

John 14:6 (NASB)

Our culture makes it hard for us to think that there can be one absolute and universal truth that applies to all people everywhere at all times.

But logic clearly demonstrates that this is the case. When we die, we'll all experience the same thing: either we'll all cease to exist, or we'll all stand before God, or we will all experience some other thing.

Believing something does not make it true and not believing something does not make it untrue. Truth is true regardless of what we choose to believe.

Is it important to you to find the truth? Why or why not?

Do you believe that there is such a thing as truth that is true for everyone at all times in all places? Why do you think this concept makes some people uncomfortable?

How does the statement that Jesus is the way, the truth and the life (John 14:6) make you feel? Why? How might you approach sharing this with others?

Faith is a choice

> Jesus Christ is the same yesterday and today and forever.
>
> **Hebrews 13:8**
>
> "If you have faith as small as a mustard seed, you can say to this mountain, 'Move from here to there,' and it will move. Nothing will be impossible for you."
>
> **Matthew 17:20**
>
> In the same way, faith by itself, if it is not accompanied by action, is dead. But someone will say, "You have faith; I have deeds." Show me your faith without deeds, and I will show you my faith by my deeds.
>
> **James 2:17–18**

Faith is simply making a choice to believe what God says is true. It's about bringing your belief system into line with what is already true.

The effectiveness of your faith is not determined by how strong it feels but by the strength and reliability of the one you put your faith in.

Growing in faith is about growing in relationship with God – as we get to know Him better, we'll trust Him more.

Faith:

Faith grows when you make a choice to believe what God says is true, stand firm on that, and step out into action.

How does the realization that faith is simply a choice you make change the way you feel about God and your daily life?

How could you get to know God better?

Would you like to take the opportunity to commit to spending more time with God? Take a moment to ask God to help you work out how best to make more time to grow in your relationship with Him. Pray for one another.

In the tough times

> And we know that in all things God works for the good of those who love him, who have been called according to his purpose.
>
> **Romans 8:28 (ESV)**

God will make good come even from our struggles.

When we learn to follow God rather than our feelings when times get tough, we will grow in our relationship with God.

"Never doubt in the dark what God told you in the light." Raymond Edman.

The Can Do List

1. Why should I say I can't do it when the Bible says I can do all things through Jesus who gives me strength (Philippians 4:13)?
2. Why should I lack when I know that God will supply all my needs according to His riches in glory in Jesus (Philippians 4:19)?
3. Why should I be afraid when the Bible says God has not given me a spirit of fear, but one of power, love, and a sound mind (2 Timothy 1:7)?
4. Why should I lack faith to complete my calling knowing that God has given me a measure of faith (Romans 12:3)?
5. Why should I be weak when the Bible says that God is the strength of my life and that I will be strong and take action because I know Him (Psalm 27:1; Daniel 11:32)?
6. Why should I allow Satan supremacy in my life when He that is in me is greater than he that is in the world (1 John 4:4)?
7. Why should I accept defeat when the Bible says that God always leads me in victory (2 Corinthians 2:14)?
8. Why should I be without wisdom when Christ became wisdom to me from God and God gives me wisdom generously when I ask Him for it (1 Corinthians 1:30; James 1:5)?
9. Why should I be depressed when I can remember God's loving kindness, compassion and faithfulness and have hope (Lamentations 3:21–23)?

10. Why should I worry when I can cast all my anxiety on Jesus who cares for me (1 Peter 5:7)?
11. Why should I ever be in bondage when I know that, where the Spirit of God is, there is freedom (2 Corinthians 3:17; Galatians 5:1)?
12. Why should I feel guilty when the Bible says I am not guilty because I am in Jesus (Romans 8:1)?
13. Why should I feel alone when Jesus said He is with me always and He will never leave me or let me go (Matthew 28:20; Hebrews 13:5)?
14. Why should I feel cursed or that I am the victim of bad luck when the Bible says that Jesus redeemed me from the curse of the law that I can receive His Spirit (Galatians 3:13–14)?
15. Why should I be discontent when, like Paul, I can learn to be content in all my circumstances (Philippians 4:11)?
16. Why should I feel worthless when Jesus became sin for me so that I could become the righteousness of God in Him (2 Corinthians 5:21)?
17. Why should I have a persecution complex knowing that nobody can be against me when God is for me (Romans 8:31)?
18. Why should I be confused when God is the author of peace and gives me knowledge through the Holy Spirit who lives in me (1 Corinthians 14:33; 1 Corinthians 2:12)?
19. Why should I feel like a failure when I am a conqueror in all things through Jesus (Romans 8:37)?
20. Why should I let the pressures of life bother me when I can take courage knowing that Jesus has overcome the world and its tribulations (John 16:33)?

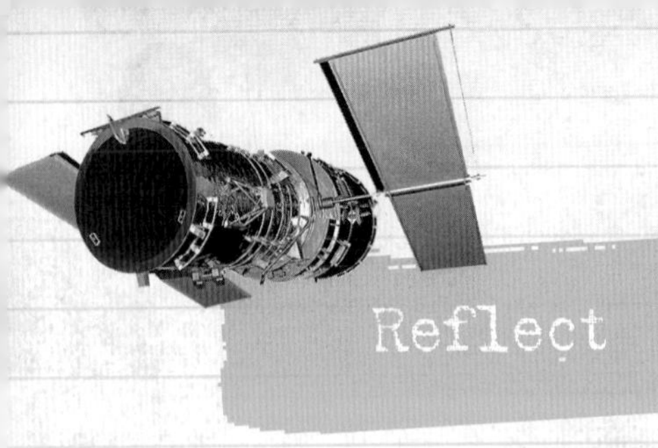

Reflect

Read "The Can Do List" out loud. Even better, find a partner and read it to each other changing "I" to "You".

Which three truths most stand out to you? Write them below. Share with each other why you have selected these particular ones.

Do you know someone who is really struggling at the moment? How could you come alongside them and show them that they are loved? Spend some time praying for them.

When you realize that an area in your belief system is not in line with what God says is true, remember to write it down on pages 190–191 together with the corresponding truth.

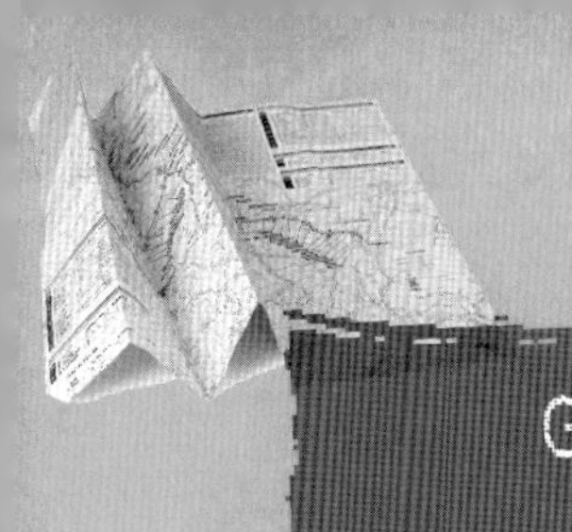

Going deeper

Read "The Can Do List" out loud slowly, letting each one sink in. Look up the corresponding verses in your Bible for the three that stand out to you the most. You could write the verses out and pin them up somewhere you will see them every day.

Life can be hard at times for all of us. If you have stuff that you're finding tough at the moment, tell God about it. See if He has anything to say to you about it.

If you're really struggling, seek out a Christian friend or pastor who can support you and pray with you.

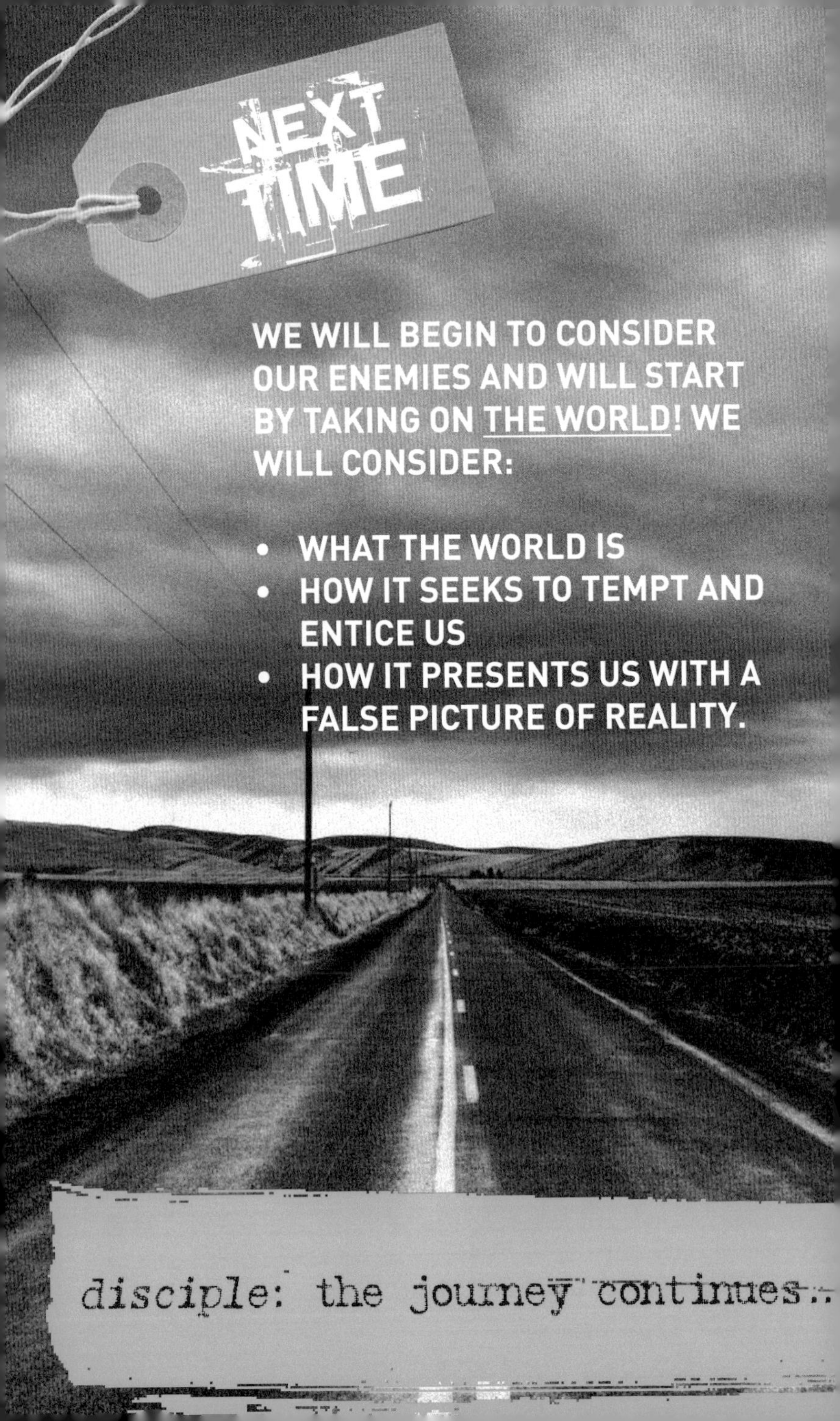
NEXT TIME
WE WILL BEGIN TO CONSIDER OUR ENEMIES AND WILL START BY TAKING ON THE WORLD! WE WILL CONSIDER:
• WHAT THE WORLD IS
• HOW IT SEEKS TO TEMPT AND ENTICE US
• HOW IT PRESENTS US WITH A FALSE PICTURE OF REALITY.
disciple: the journey continues...

04

The story of the world

WHY?

Do not conform to the pattern of this world, but be transformed by the renewing of your mind. Then you will be able to test and approve what God's will is – his good, pleasing and perfect will.

Romans 12:2

The world seeks to knock us off track and redirect our life stories away from the plans that God has for us through false promises, consumerism, and comfort, and by presenting us with a false picture of reality.

How would you feel if you were deprived of the ability to go online or use your favourite media?

If you were in charge of marketing some new consumer product (maybe a clothing range, a new electronic gizmo, or a luxury foodstuff) what message would you put in your advertising to try to persuade people they need it?

1

False promises

"I do not ask that you take them out of the world, but that you keep them from the evil one. They are not of the world, just as I am not of the world. Sanctify them in the truth; your word is truth."

John 17:15–17 (ESV)

Satan is the ruler of the world (John 12:31, 14:30) and is behind its false promises to us.

The world promises to meet our needs for significance, acceptance and security and says:

- **Perform well + Accomplish = Significance**
- **Status + Wealth = Security**
- **Good Image + Admiration = Acceptance**

Seeking comfort and consumerism exert a huge subliminal pull on us.

The world's promises are bankrupt and count for nothing eternally.

Ctrl+C

DO NOT STORE UP FOR YOURSELVES TREASURES ON EARTH, WHERE MOTHS AND VERMIN DESTROY, AND WHERE THIEVES BREAK IN AND STEAL. BUT STORE UP FOR YOURSELVES TREASURES IN HEAVEN, WHERE MOTHS AND VERMIN DO NOT DESTROY, AND WHERE THIEVES DO NOT BREAK IN AND STEAL.

Matthew 6:19–20

How have you seen the world's false promises at play in life? How do these false promises shape the way society views someone who has nothing – a homeless person on the street for example?

Have you ever fallen for the idea that having the right "stuff" marks you out as having "made it" or being worth "knowing"? How? What can we do to counter this idea in our lives?

Which of the three false promises are you most vulnerable to? How can you combat it in your daily life?

2 Distractions and enticements

> Do not love the world or anything in the world. If anyone loves the world, love for the Father is not in them. For everything in the world – the lust of the flesh, the lust of the eyes and the pride of life – comes not from the Father but from the world. The world and its desires pass away, but whoever does the will of God lives forever.
>
> **1 John 2:15–17**

The lust of the flesh, the lust of the eyes, and the pride of life seek to entice us but lead to nothing but darkness and bondage.

Lust of the flesh = the pull on our bodies to form unhelpful habits like comfort eating and sleeping around.

Lust of the eyes = when we lose ourselves in screens looking at pornography, horror, or celebrities.

Pride of life = the pull on our egos to achieve and boast.

DO YOU NOT KNOW THAT HE WHO IS JOINED TO A PROSTITUTE BECOMES ONE BODY WITH HER? FOR, AS IT IS WRITTEN, "THE TWO WILL BECOME ONE FLESH."

1 Corinthians 6:16

"THE EYE IS THE LAMP OF THE BODY. IF YOUR EYES ARE HEALTHY, YOUR WHOLE BODY WILL BE FULL OF LIGHT. BUT IF YOUR EYES ARE UNHEALTHY, YOUR WHOLE BODY WILL BE FULL OF DARKNESS."

Matthew 6:22–23

BUT HE GIVES US MORE GRACE. THAT IS WHY SCRIPTURE SAYS: "GOD OPPOSES THE PROUD BUT SHOWS FAVOUR TO THE HUMBLE."

James 4:6

"Sex is a beautiful gift from God when it is enjoyed in the way He intended?" Do you agree with this statement? Why or why not? (Note: if you want to know more about this, when you get home you can watch an extra teaching film on it via the app).

How do you feel about the idea that what you look at can affect your spiritual health? What practical things could you do to protect your spiritual health with regard to this?

"Though the LORD is great, he cares for the humble, but he keeps his distance from the proud." (Psalm 138:6, NLT). Why do you think pride is so abhorrent to God?

3

False reality

"I am the way, and the truth, and the life; no one comes to the Father but through Me."

John 14:6 (NASB)

Do not conform to the pattern of this world, but be transformed by the renewing of your mind.

Romans 12:2

We all inherit from our culture a way of making sense of reality but our worldview paints a false picture of reality.

God tells us in the Bible what reality is actually like. When we adopt the "biblical worldview" we will see the world as it really is.

We need to critically evaluate the views that we have absorbed from our culture and environment to make sure that we do not have a "salad bar" or "pick 'n' mix" faith.

Reflect

It can be very difficult to realize that we have a worldview. Use this time to help each other grasp this by considering these questions:

- If you had been born thirty years earlier, how would the way you look at the world have been different? If you had been born thirty years later, do you think it would be different again?
- If you had been born in a different culture, how might the way you see life be different?
- What does this tell you about whether or not your worldview is accurately representing reality?
- Are you able to identify areas where you have taken a "salad bar" or "pick 'n' mix" approach to faith, that is, where you have chosen to overlook some things that God says in His Word?

When you realize that an area in your belief system is not in line with what God says is true, remember to write it down on pages 190–191 together with the corresponding truth.

Going deeper

Remember, the battle we are in takes place in our minds and is a battle between truth and lies. Start by saying a prayer to dedicate yourself to seeing reality as God says it is.

Have you realized that you have been trusting your traditional worldview more than God's Word? If so, spend some time in prayer rejecting your worldview and committing yourself to the Biblical worldview.

Ask God to show you what things in the world entice you most effectively. Consider how you can make it less likely that you will fall for their deception.

ON THE APP

THE GIFT OF SEX

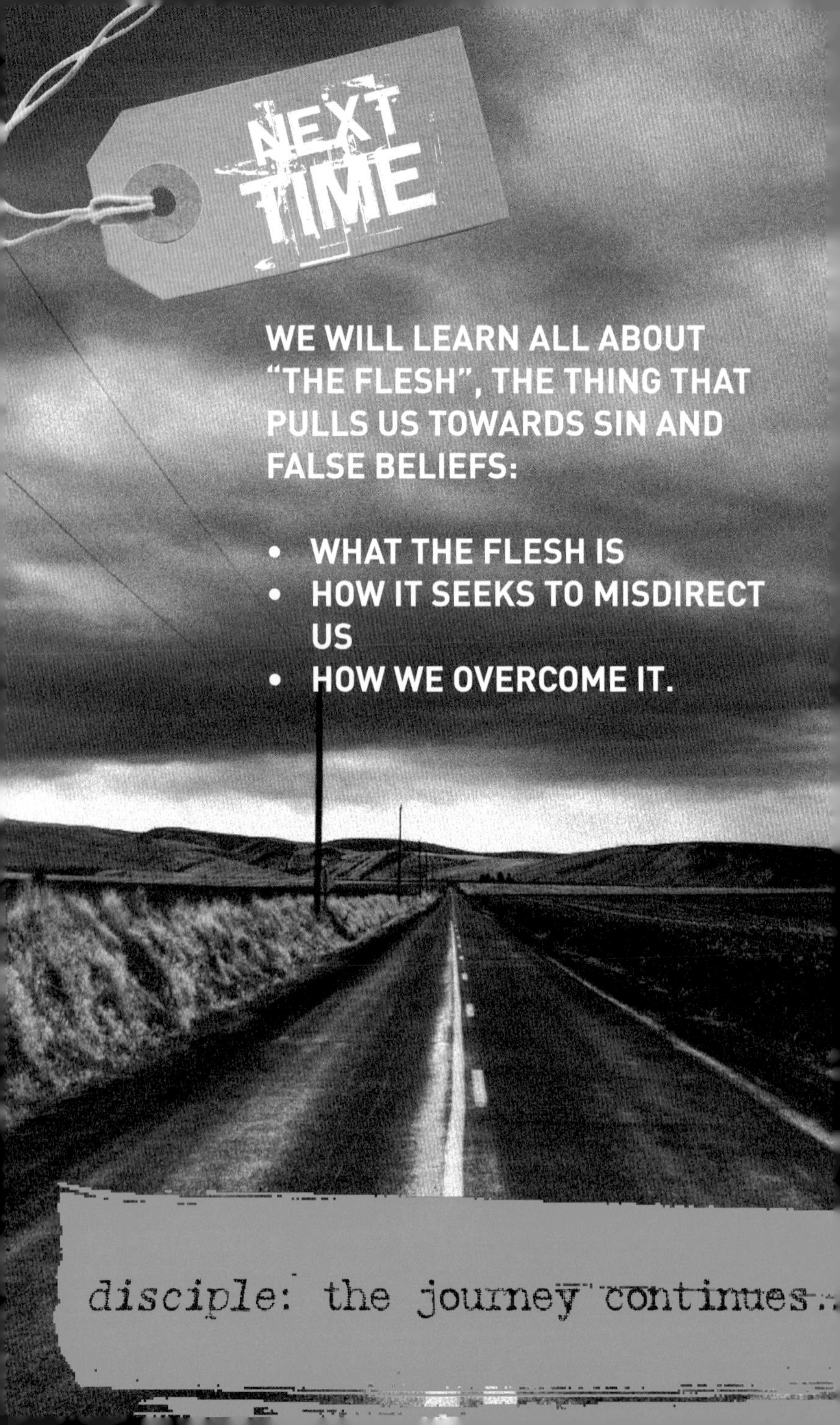
NEXT TIME
WE WILL LEARN ALL ABOUT "THE FLESH", THE THING THAT PULLS US TOWARDS SIN AND FALSE BELIEFS:
• WHAT THE FLESH IS
• HOW IT SEEKS TO MISDIRECT US
• HOW WE OVERCOME IT.
disciple: the journey continues...

05

The story of the flesh

You, however, are not in the flesh but in the Spirit, if in fact the Spirit of God dwells in you.

Romans 8:9 (ESV)

The weapons we fight with are not the weapons of the world. On the contrary, they have divine power to demolish strongholds.

2 Corinthians 10:4

The flesh is what comes naturally to a fallen human being. It consists of beliefs and thoughts that are contrary to God's truth that pull us towards sin and hopelessness.

Although we became new creations and holy ones when we turned to Jesus, no one pressed a "delete" button in our minds. Those unhelpful ways of thinking are still there. We do, however, have everything we need to overcome the flesh. But it requires some effort and persistence.

Which people from your past have had the most positive influence on who you are today?

What people or experiences from your past have had the most negative impact on how you see yourself?

Understanding the flesh

> Those who live according to the flesh have their minds set on what the flesh desires; but those who live in accordance with the Spirit have their minds set on what the Spirit desires. The mind governed by the flesh is death, but the mind governed by the Spirit is life and peace.
>
> **Romans 8:5–7**

Christianity is not a quick-fix. Becoming like Jesus is a process that takes time and effort. We need to be intentional about becoming a fruitful disciple.

When we became Christians we changed but the pull of the flesh didn't disappear.

Being a disciple is not about everything in life being easy and feeling good. It's about a relationship with God who promises to help you through whatever life throws at you and make your life count for eternity.

If the flesh is "what comes naturally to a fallen human" or "default programming", can you think of some of the ways it shows up in your life or in other people's lives?

Where do you tend to look for comfort when life is tough or things go wrong?

Do you recognize in your own life or in other people's lives the tendency to believe the lie that says "the goal of being a Christian is to feel good and be happy"? What are the dangers of falling for this lie?

2

Natural, spiritual or fleshly?

Through Christ Jesus the law of the Spirit who gives life has set you free from the law of sin and death.

Romans 8:2

So I say, walk by the Spirit, and you will not gratify the desires of the flesh.

Galatians 5:16

His divine power has given us everything we need for a godly life through our knowledge of him who called us by his own glory and goodness.

2 Peter 1:3

Paul categorizes all people into three types:

- The natural person is a not-yet-Christian, someone who is spiritually dead.
- The spiritual person lives by the Spirit and crucifies their flesh daily (see Galatians 5:22–23).
- The fleshly person is a Christian who is living in contradiction to their new identity in Christ and whose life looks more like that of a not-yet-Christian.

Living as a spiritual person is perfectly possible, indeed it should be our expectation. But we can be held back by:

- Not knowing the truth
- Deception
- Unresolved personal or spiritual issues.

"The law of sin and death" is still in force and pulls us towards sin but we can choose to overcome it by a greater law – the law of the Spirit of life!

THE **NATURAL PERSON** DOES NOT ACCEPT THE THINGS OF THE SPIRIT OF GOD, FOR THEY ARE FOLLY TO HIM, AND HE IS NOT ABLE TO UNDERSTAND THEM BECAUSE THEY ARE SPIRITUALLY DISCERNED. THE **SPIRITUAL PERSON** JUDGES ALL THINGS, BUT IS HIMSELF TO BE JUDGED BY NO ONE. "FOR WHO HAS UNDERSTOOD THE MIND OF THE LORD SO AS TO INSTRUCT HIM?" BUT WE HAVE THE MIND OF CHRIST.

BUT I, BROTHERS, COULD NOT ADDRESS YOU AS SPIRITUAL PEOPLE, BUT AS **PEOPLE OF THE FLESH**, AS INFANTS IN CHRIST. I FED YOU WITH MILK, NOT SOLID FOOD, FOR YOU WERE NOT READY FOR IT. AND EVEN NOW YOU ARE NOT YET READY, FOR YOU ARE STILL OF THE FLESH. FOR WHILE THERE IS JEALOUSY AND STRIFE AMONG YOU, ARE YOU NOT OF THE FLESH AND BEHAVING ONLY IN A HUMAN WAY?

1 Corinthians 2:14 – 3:3 (ESV)

Look at 1 Corinthians 2:14–3:3 (on page 81). Which type of person would you say you are: a natural person (does not yet know Jesus); a spiritual person (knows Jesus and walks by the Spirit); or a fleshly person (knows Jesus but walks by the flesh)?

Which type of person would you like to be?

Do you agree that living as a spiritual person is not some unattainable ideal but perfectly possible for every Christian? Why or why not?

3 Living by the Spirit

"Come to me, all you who are weary and burdened, and I will give you rest. Take my yoke upon you and learn from me, for I am gentle and humble in heart, and you will find rest for your souls."

Matthew 11:28–29

The fruit of the Spirit is love, joy, peace, forbearance, kindness, goodness, faithfulness, gentleness and self-control.

Galatians 5:22–23

No temptation has overtaken you except what is common to mankind. And God is faithful; he will not let you be tempted beyond what you can bear. But when you are tempted, he will also provide a way out so that you can endure it.

1 Corinthians 10:13

Living by the Spirit is a choice we make which is born out of our relationship with God.

If we continue to make good choices, we will automatically bear fruit. The fruit of the Spirit is all to do with our character.

All temptation is simply an attempt to get you to meet your legitimate needs for significance, security, and acceptance independently of God. There is always a way of escape and it comes right at the start of the thought process.

Reflect

What most struck you about what living by the Spirit really is and why?

What, if anything, is holding you back from maturing into the fruitful disciple God has created you to be?

Pray for each other. Why not take this opportunity to make a commitment to God and yourself to see this course through to the end?

When you realize that an area in your belief system is not in line with what God says is true, remember to write it down on pages 190–191 together with the corresponding truth.

Going deeper

What temptations do you particularly struggle with?

Ask God to help you identify the thought processes that have led to you giving in to them in the past.

What would it look like to "take those thoughts captive" right at the start of the process?

Read Galatians 5:22–23 and think about those character attributes. Can you envisage them growing in your life as you continue to make good choices? How different would your life be if that happened?

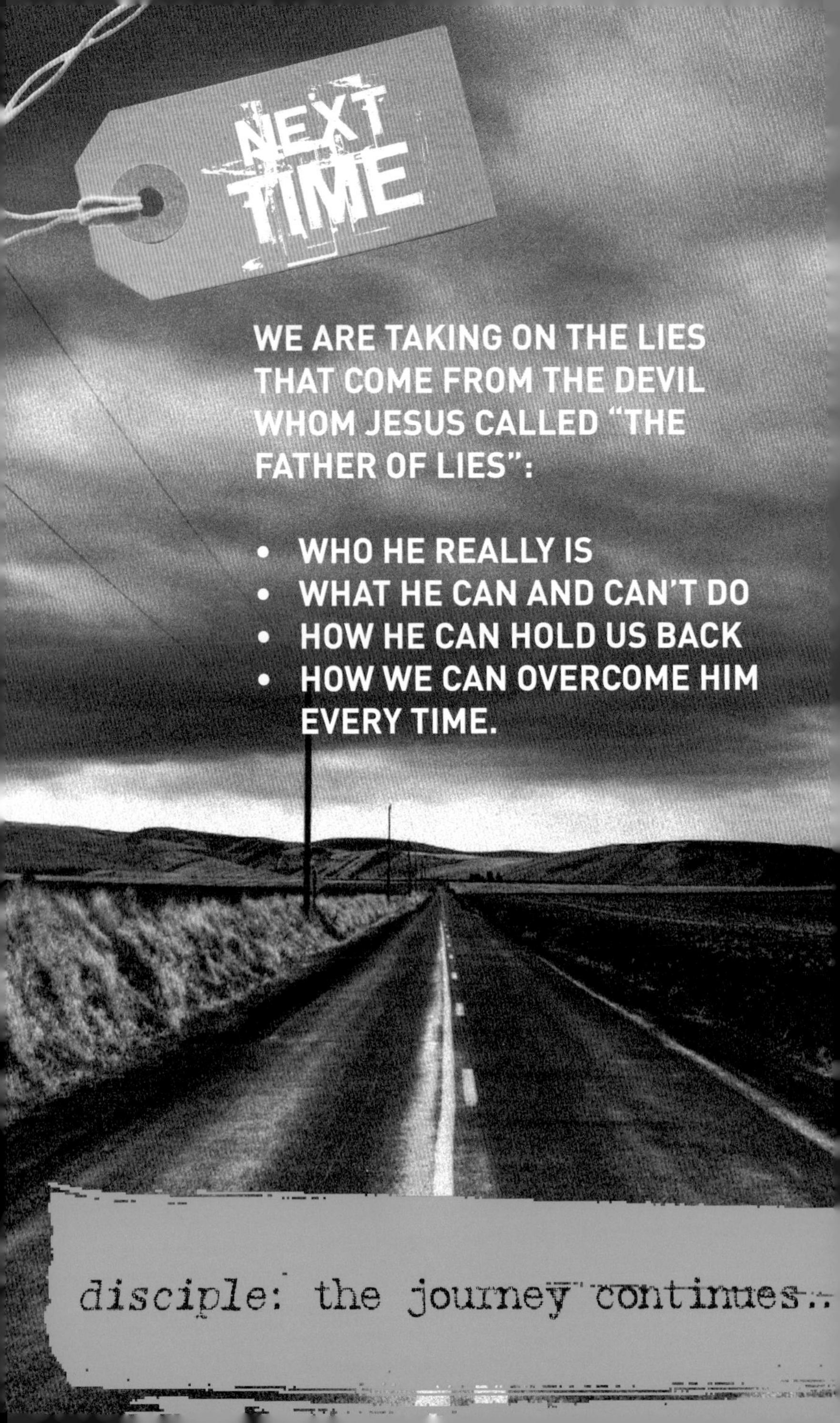
NEXT TIME
WE ARE TAKING ON THE LIES THAT COME FROM THE DEVIL WHOM JESUS CALLED "THE FATHER OF LIES":
• WHO HE REALLY IS
• WHAT HE CAN AND CAN'T DO
• HOW HE CAN HOLD US BACK
• HOW WE CAN OVERCOME HIM EVERY TIME.
disciple: the journey continues...

06

The story of the devil

> Be alert and of sober mind. Your enemy the devil prowls around like a roaring lion looking for someone to devour. Resist him, standing firm in the faith, because you know that the family of believers throughout the world is undergoing the same kind of sufferings.
>
> **1 Peter 5:8–9**

The devil is real but is a defeated foe. We already have everything we need to overcome him in our lives so that we can fulfil the amazing plans that God has for us and make our lives count. But to overcome him we need to understand who he is and how he works.

Declaration

In Jesus' name we declare that God is sovereign. We submit ourselves to God and tell every enemy of the Lord Jesus Christ to leave this place now. We declare that they cannot stop the will of God being done in this group or in our lives. We belong to Jesus and the evil one cannot touch us.

If you felt you weren't making enough progress in your walk with God and wanted to fix this, where might be a good place to start?

C. S. Lewis wrote, "There are two equal and opposite errors into which our race can fall about the devils. One is to disbelieve in their existence. The other is to believe, and to feel an excessive and unhealthy interest in them. They themselves are equally pleased by both errors, and hail a materialist or magician with the same delight." (C.S. Lewis, *The Screwtape Letters*, 1941, p. 3). Which of these two errors do you tend towards?

The devil and you

Now is the time for judgment on this world; now the prince of this world will be driven out.

John 12:31

As for you, you were dead in your transgressions and sins, in which you used to live when you followed the ways of this world and of the ruler of the kingdom of the air, the spirit who is now at work in those who are disobedient.

Ephesians 2:1–2

We know that we are children of God, and that the whole world is under the control of the evil one.

1 John 5:19

The one who does what is sinful is of the devil, because the devil has been sinning from the beginning. The reason the Son of God appeared was to destroy the devil's work.

1 John 3:8

And having disarmed the powers and authorities, he made a public spectacle of them, triumphing over them by the cross.

Colossians 2:15

Then Jesus came to them and said, "All authority in heaven and on earth has been given to me. Therefore go and make disciples of all nations, baptizing them in the name of the Father and of the Son and of the Holy Spirit, and teaching them to obey everything I have commanded you. And surely I am with you always, to the very end of the age."

Matthew 28:18–20

And God raised us up with Christ and seated us with him in the heavenly realms in Christ Jesus.

Ephesians 2:6

The one who was born of God keeps them safe, and the evil one cannot harm them.

1 John 5:18

Lies, lies, lies...

[The devil] was a murderer from the beginning, not holding to the truth, for there is no truth in him. When he lies, he speaks his native language, for he is a liar and the father of lies.

John 8:44

Lie 1: He isn't real.

Lie 2: He is equal in power to God.

Lie 3: He is more powerful than we are.

Lie 4: We are immune to his tactics.

The truth is:

- Satan can do nothing to change our true identity as holy ones in Jesus Christ.
- We have much more power and authority than Satan does.
- Satan is already defeated.
- Satan's powers are NO match for God.

Satan has no power over us other than what we give him.

How hard do you find it to believe that the devil and demons are real? Why do you think that is?

Which of the four lies we looked at are you most susceptible to? What can you do about this?

Read Ephesians 6:11–18 (on the next page). What do you think it means in practice to put on the armour of God?

Put on the full armour of God, so that you can take your stand against the devil's schemes. For our struggle is not against flesh and blood, but against the rulers, against the authorities, against the powers of this dark world and against the spiritual forces of evil in the heavenly realms. Therefore put on the full armour of God, so that when the day of evil comes, you may be able to stand your ground, and after you have done everything, to stand. Stand firm then, with the belt of truth buckled around your waist, with the breastplate of righteousness in place, and with your feet fitted with the readiness that comes from the gospel of peace. In addition to all this, take up the shield of faith, with which you can extinguish all the flaming arrows of the evil one. Take the helmet of salvation and the sword of the Spirit, which is the word of God. And pray in the Spirit on all occasions with all kinds of prayers and requests. With this in mind, be alert and always keep on praying for all the Lord's people.

Ephesians 6:11–18

2

The devil's tactics

"In your anger do not sin": Do not let the sun go down while you are still angry, and do not give the devil a foothold.

Ephesians 4:26–27

Submit yourselves, then, to God. Resist the devil, and he will flee from you.

James 4:7

The Spirit clearly says that in later times some will abandon the faith and follow deceiving spirits and things taught by demons.

1 Timothy 4:1

Satan has only three tactics: to tempt, to accuse, and to deceive.

Temptation

Remember, temptation is an attempt to get you to meet your legitimate need for significance, security, and acceptance outside of God.

If we fall for temptation we give the devil a foothold.

Although a Christian can allow the enemy some influence in their life through sin they can never become completely taken over ("possessed") by demons. At our very core is the Holy Spirit. We belong to God and Satan can never take us back.

Accusation
This comes once we've succumbed to temptation – like a double punch.

We need to know that there really is no condemnation for us, at least not from God, the only one who matters! (See Romans 8:1).

Deception
By definition, we don't know when we are being deceived.

Our greatest weapon is knowing the truth of God's word.

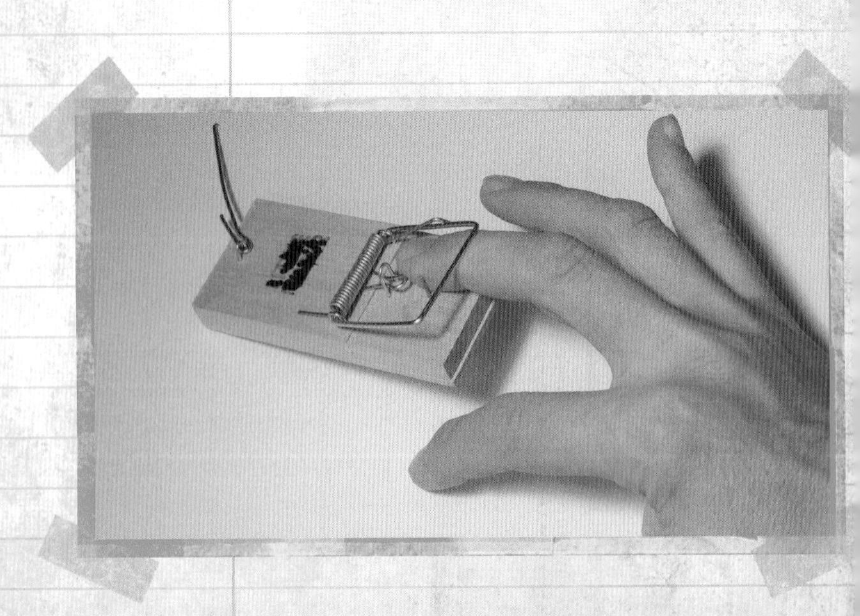

Footholds:

We give the devil footholds through sin. The way to resolve them is to submit to God through repentance and then resist him. At that point he has to <u>FLEE</u> from us. See James 4:7.

Does it surprise you to learn that not every thought that comes into your mind is your own? Is it more important to work out where a thought is coming from or to test it to see whether or not it is true?

Read Ephesians 4:26–27. What do you think the effects of giving the devil a foothold in your life would actually look like in everyday life?

If you are being deceived, by definition you don't know it. Share some examples of ways you have been deceived by the enemy in the past. How can you uncover ways he may be deceiving you right now?

3

Stand firm!

> I will build my church, and the gates of hell shall not prevail against it.
>
> **Matthew 16:18b (ESV)**

Our defence is knowing the truth of God's word and putting on the armour of God.

We have no reason to fear the devil, or go on demon hunts.

We need to know about the devil and demons and how they work so that we can take the necessary precautions. But we don't need to focus on them – we focus on Jesus and living a righteous life.

We are not called to drive out the darkness – we are called to turn on the light!

Reflect

Deception is Satan's most effective tactic because if you are being deceived, by definition you don't know about it!

Do you think it is possible that you are being deceived right now?

Pray for each other in pairs – that the Holy Spirit would lead you into all truth, especially as you prepare to go through *The Steps To Freedom In Christ* soon where you will be able to deal with the things that are holding you back.

When you realize that an area in your belief system is not in line with what God says is true, remember to write it down on pages 190–191 together with the corresponding truth.

Going deeper

How does the enemy tend to tempt you?

How does he tend to accuse you?

If you are struggling to work these out, ask God to show you.

What will you do next time the tempting or accusing thoughts come? Are there any Bible verses that would be helpful for you to remember? You could write them out and pin them up somewhere to remind you.

ON THE APP

THE TRUTH BEHIND THE OCCULT

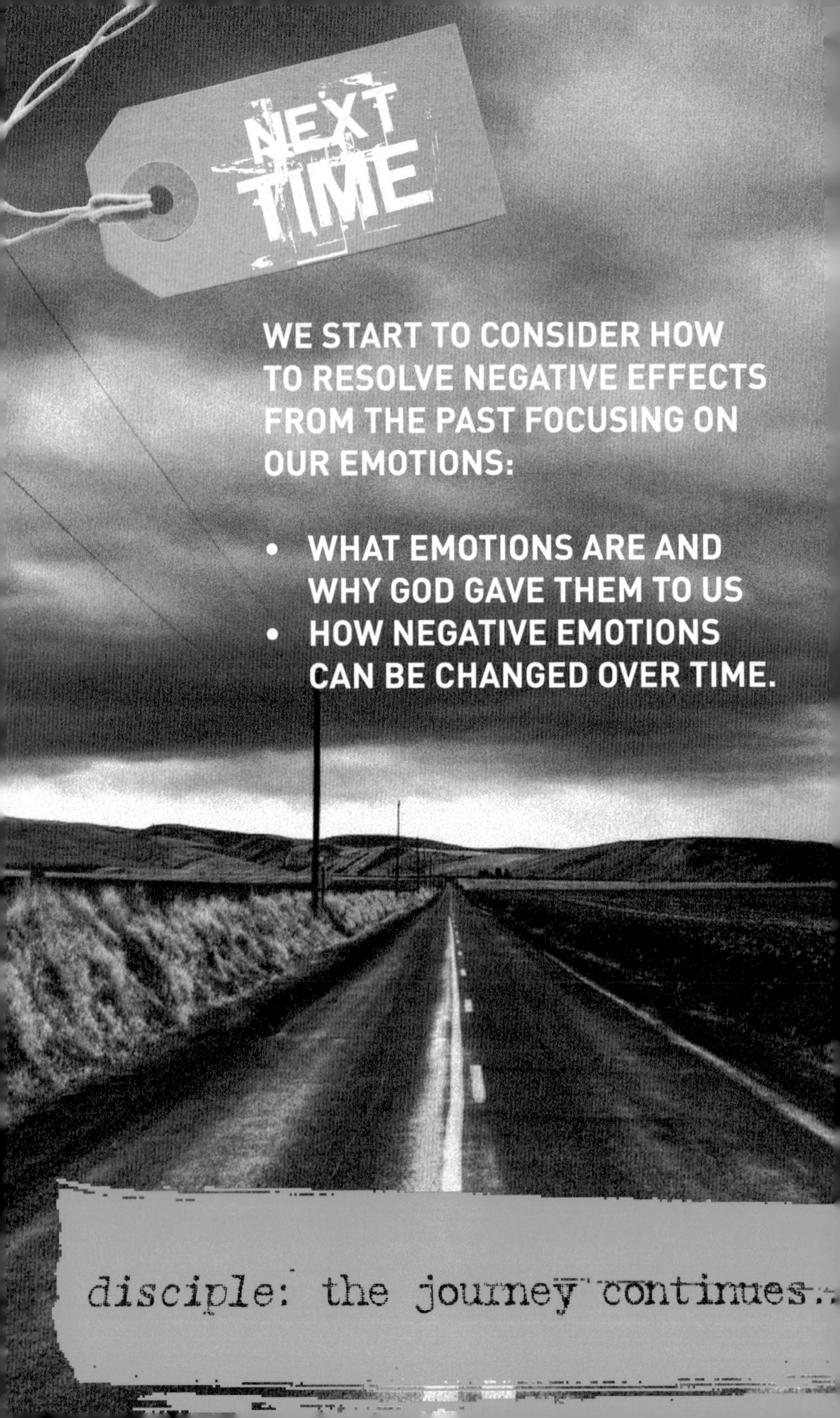
NEXT TIME
WE START TO CONSIDER HOW TO RESOLVE NEGATIVE EFFECTS FROM THE PAST FOCUSING ON OUR EMOTIONS:
• WHAT EMOTIONS ARE AND WHY GOD GAVE THEM TO US
• HOW NEGATIVE EMOTIONS CAN BE CHANGED OVER TIME.
disciple: the journey continues..

07

Truth and emotions

WHY?

"In your anger do not sin": do not let the sun go down while you are still angry, and do not give the devil a foothold."

Ephesians 4:26–27

Cast all your anxiety on him because he cares for you. Be alert and of sober mind. Your enemy the devil prowls around like a roaring lion looking for someone to devour.

1 Peter 5:7–8

Note the link between emotions (anger and anxiety) and giving ground in our lives to the devil in the now-familiar passages above.

Our emotions are given to us by God and serve as barometers of our spiritual health. It's essential to heed what they tell us and make adjustments when necessary if we want to stay on track.

Declaration

In Jesus' name we declare that God is sovereign in this place and over our lives and we submit ourselves to Him. We declare that we are here by legal right and that every enemy of the Lord Jesus Christ must be silent and leave this place immediately.

Have your emotions ever run away with you? Or has there ever been a time when you wished you could have let your emotions run away with you a little more than you did? What happened?

Do you think, on balance, that our emotions are a good thing or a bad thing? Why? If you agree that they were given to us by God, what purpose do you think He had in mind for them?

What are our emotions?

> "I will never leave you nor forsake you."
> **Hebrews 13:5 (ESV)**

Emotions are given to us by God as a gift for our own good but it's easy to trust them rather than the truth in God's Word.

Emotions act as signposts to what is happening in our soul. Negative emotions are to your inner person what the ability to feel physical pain is to your body.

When we feel angry, anxious, or depressed, it may be a sign that something in our belief system is not right and that we have some adjustments to make.

Depression

In case you're wondering and just to be absolutely clear, we are not saying that all depression comes from faulty beliefs or goals that feel unreachable (see page 152). It can also be caused by biochemical issues. However, if you suffer from depression, we'd certainly recommend looking at your beliefs and goals before God to make sure that they are not a contributory factor.

Our generation stands accused of believing that the most important goal in life is personal happiness. In what ways do you recognize this in your own life or in the lives of those around you?

What are the dangers of making choices based on our feelings?

Having listened to what Rob has said, have you changed your opinion about whether your emotions are a good thing or a bad thing? Why or why not?

Can we change the way we feel?

When Saul and all Israel heard these words of the Philistine, they were dismayed and greatly afraid.

1 Samuel 17:11 (ESV)

"The Lord who delivered me from the paw of the lion and from the paw of the bear will deliver me from the hand of this Philistine."

1 Samuel 17:37 (ESV)

We can learn to manage our emotions but it takes time.

If what we believe doesn't reflect truth, our feelings won't reflect reality.

Life events don't determine how you feel but your perception of them does.

We are tempted to suppress our emotions or express them indiscriminately but God wants us to be emotionally real and honest (as David was in the prayer on page 112).

By making a choice to believe God's truth rather than our emotions, we'll find that our emotions will (eventually) line up with what's really true.

What on earth is this doing in the Bible?

Appoint someone evil to oppose my enemy; let an accuser stand at his right hand. When he is tried, let him be found guilty, and may his prayers condemn him. May his days be few; may another take his place of leadership. May his children be fatherless and his wife a widow. May his children be wandering beggars; may they be driven from their ruined homes. May a creditor seize all he has; may strangers plunder the fruits of his labour. May no one extend kindness to him or take pity on his fatherless children. May his descendants be cut off, their names blotted out from the next generation. May the iniquity of his fathers be remembered before the LORD; may the sin of his mother never be blotted out. May their sins always remain before the LORD, that he may blot out their name from the earth.

Psalm 109:6–15

Have you ever felt like that? Have you ever prayed like that?
Would it be right to pray like that?
Was God surprised or did He already know David felt this way?
Is He big enough to take a bit of a temper tantrum from us?
Why did He inspire David to write it down and put it in the Bible?

Talk about a time when your wrong perception of a situation caused you to get into an unnecessary emotional state.

What "Goliaths" do you have to face? How much bigger than your Goliaths is God? What can you do to ensure you see the situation as it really is?

Have a look at the passage from the Psalms on the previous page and discuss the questions below it.

3

Roots

> Hear me, Lord, and answer me, for I am poor and needy. Guard my life, for I am faithful to you; save your servant who trusts in you. You are my God; have mercy on me, Lord, for I call to you all day long. Bring joy to your servant, Lord, for I put my trust in you.
>
> **Psalm 86:1–4**

The negative emotions that plague us today often have their roots in our past. But it's not so much what happened to us in the past that's the problem – it's the lies we believe as a result of what happened.

What we feel and how we behave are dictated by what we REALLY believe in our hearts.

As children of God, we are not a product of our past. We are a product of Jesus' past – His life, death, resurrection, and ascension.

We don't feel our way into good behaviour – we behave our way into good feelings.

No one has a backstory too messed up to find their complete freedom and make their life count.

Reflect

- What struck you most in this session?
- What emotions do you most struggle with?
- What unhelpful way do you most tend to respond to your own emotions; ignore them, or explode?
- How does it make you feel to think that your past doesn't have to hold you back any more?

Spend some time praying for each other.

When you realize that an area in your belief system is not in line with what God says is true, remember to write it down on pages 190–191 together with the corresponding truth.

Going deeper

Many people have stuff in their past that they don't want to think about again. But walking in freedom means looking at it again with the comforting Holy Spirit so that you can recognize the lies you have come to believe and take steps to believe the truth instead. Remember, life's events don't determine how you feel but your perception of them does.

- Is there something in your past that you have been trying to hide from? Bring it to God in prayer. Ask God to show you what it caused you to believe about yourself or Him that may not actually be true. And ask Him to lead you into freedom from it once and for all as you continue through the course.

- If you are struggling with difficult emotions at the moment, tell God exactly how you're feeling, and ask Him to help you. It may be helpful to find a Christian friend or church leader who can help you if you're really struggling.

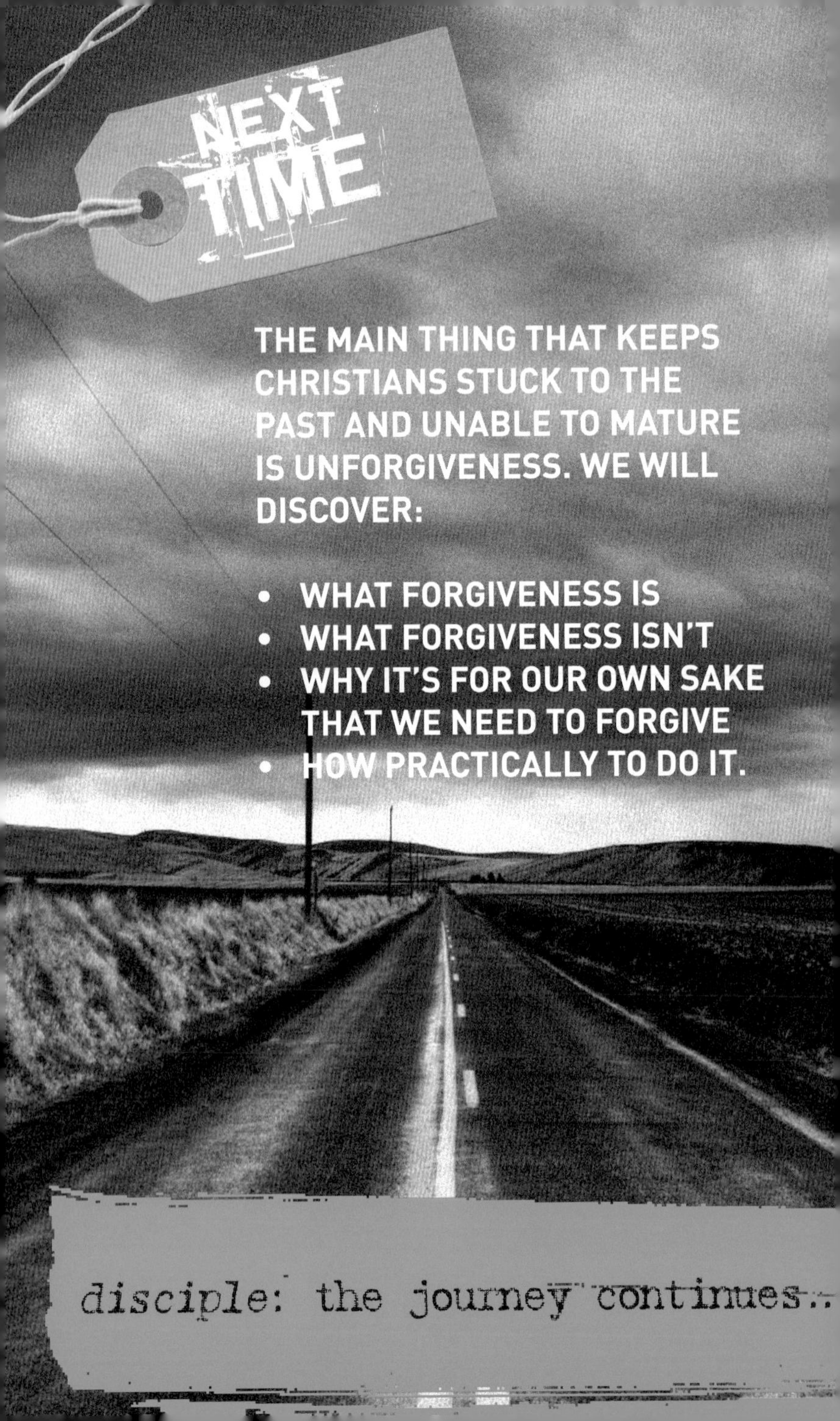
NEXT TIME
THE MAIN THING THAT KEEPS CHRISTIANS STUCK TO THE PAST AND UNABLE TO MATURE IS UNFORGIVENESS. WE WILL DISCOVER:
• WHAT FORGIVENESS IS
• WHAT FORGIVENESS ISN'T
• WHY IT'S FOR OUR OWN SAKE THAT WE NEED TO FORGIVE
• HOW PRACTICALLY TO DO IT.
disciple: the journey continues...

08

Forgiving from the heart

"'Shouldn't you have had mercy on your fellow servant just as I had on you?' In anger his master handed him over to the jailers to be tortured, until he should pay back all he owed. This is how my heavenly Father will treat each of you unless you forgive your brother or sister from your heart."

Matthew 18:33–35

Most of us have not been taught what forgiveness really is and that it is for our own spiritual wellbeing that God commands us to forgive.

Declaration

I declare that my mind is my own and is to be a quiet place just for me and Jesus. I submit myself to God and I command – I don't suggest – I command every enemy of the Lord Jesus Christ to leave my presence immediately.

What other examples do you know where someone has exhibited radical forgiveness?

Do you think you could forgive someone completely for something as serious as Tamsin described in the film? Why or why not?

1

Why should I?

Be merciful, just as your Father is merciful.

Luke 6:36

Forgive us our sins, for we also forgive everyone who sins against us.

Luke 11:4

Anyone you forgive, I also forgive. And what I have forgiven – if there was anything to forgive – I have forgiven in the sight of Christ for your sake, in order that Satan might not outwit us. For we are not unaware of his schemes.

2 Corinthians 2:10–11

We forgive because God forgave us and because He commands us to do the same.

As we have seen, unforgiveness allows the devil a foothold (a place of influence) in our lives and can allow him to outwit us.

When we don't forgive, even though we ourselves have been forgiven, we become just like the unforgiving servant in Jesus' story and can suffer spiritual torment as a consequence.

The unforgiving servant

"Therefore, the kingdom of heaven is like a king who wanted to settle accounts with his servants. As he began the settlement, a man who owed him ten thousand talents was brought to him. Since he was not able to pay, the master ordered that he and his wife and his children and all that he had be sold to repay the debt.

"At this the servant fell on his knees before him. 'Be patient with me,' he begged, 'and I will pay back everything.' The servant's master took pity on him, cancelled the debt and let him go.

"But when that servant went out, he found one of his fellow servants who owed him a hundred silver coins. He grabbed him and began to choke him. 'Pay back what you owe me!' he demanded.

"His fellow servant fell to his knees and begged him, 'Be patient with me, and I will pay it back.'

"But he refused. Instead, he went off and had the man thrown into prison until he could pay the debt. When the other servants saw what had happened, they were outraged and went and told their master everything that had happened.

"Then the master called the servant in. 'You wicked servant,' he said, 'I cancelled all that debt of yours because you begged me to. Shouldn't you have had mercy on your fellow servant just as I had on you?' In anger his master handed him over to the jailers to be tortured, until he should pay back all he owed.

"This is how my heavenly Father will treat each of you unless you forgive your brother or sister from your heart."

Matthew 18:23-35

JUSTICE: Giving you what you deserve.

MERCY: Not giving you what you deserve.

GRACE: Giving you what you don't deserve.

How much have you been forgiven by God through Jesus? How might knowing this help you to forgive others?

How does God square the circle of the requirement for justice for all sins? To put it another way, how is God able to forgive us even though His righteous character demands that the debt of our sin is repaid?

2

What is forgiveness?

Submit yourselves for the Lord's sake to every human authority: whether to the emperor, as the supreme authority, or to governors, who are sent by him to punish those who do wrong and to commend those who do right.

1 Peter 2:13–14

Do not take revenge, my dear friends, but leave room for God's wrath, for it is written: "It is mine to avenge; I will repay," says the Lord.

Romans 12:19

Forgiveness is not forgetting what happened or saying it was OK.

Neither is it tolerating continual sin: you can forgive someone and still report them to the authorities if what they have done is illegal.

Forgiveness is not seeking revenge. It is taking a step of faith to hand it all over to God and trusting Him to make things right on our behalf. It means believing Him when He says, "I will repay". We make a choice to leave it in His hands so that we can walk away in freedom, no longer needing to seek revenge.

So, forgiveness is not forgetting, it's not tolerating sin, and it's not seeking revenge. How will knowing this help you to forgive those who have hurt you?

Does it surprise you that God promises you justice? How does this make it possible to forgive the people who have hurt us?

In the story we looked at in the first section, Jesus said we have to "forgive from the heart". What do you think that would look like in practice?

3

How do I do it?

> If it is possible, as far as it depends on you, live at peace with everyone.
>
> **Romans 12:18**

We have to be intentional about forgiving. We will never feel like forgiving – it's a choice we make in order to take hold of our freedom and heal our damaged emotions.

Forgiveness is an issue between us and God – you don't have to go to the person who hurt you.

Forgiveness doesn't mean you will necessarily be friends again afterwards – that does not depend entirely on you.

Forgiving means living with the consequences of their sin. But you are going to have to do that anyway. Your choice is whether to do it in the bondage of bitterness or the freedom of forgiveness.

Forgiving from the heart:

"God, I choose to forgive ________________ for ________________ which made me feel ________________."

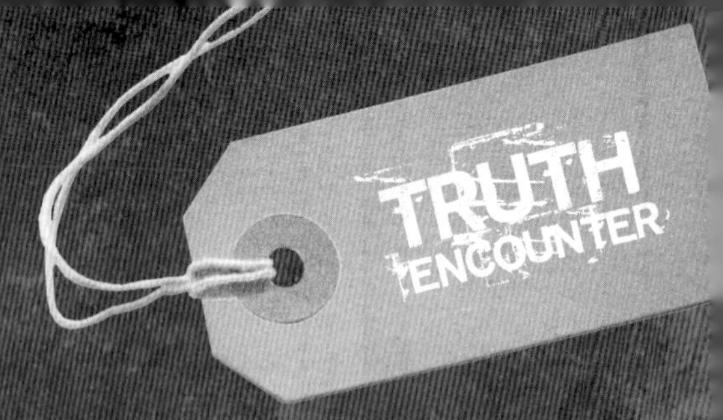

My Father God...

I renounce the lie that my Father God is distant or not interested in me.

I joyfully accept the truth that my Father God is intimate and involved (see Psalm 139:1–18).

I renounce the lie that my Father God is insensitive and uncaring.

I joyfully accept the truth that my Father God is kind and compassionate (see Psalm 103:8–14).

I renounce the lie that my Father God is strict and demanding.

I joyfully accept the truth that my Father God is accepting and filled with joy and love (see Romans 15:7; Zephaniah 3:17).

I renounce the lie that my Father God is passive and cold.

I joyfully accept the truth that my Father God is warm and affectionate (see Isaiah 40:11; Hosea 11:3–4).

I renounce the lie that my Father God is absent or too busy for me.

I joyfully accept the truth that my Father God is always with me and eager to be with me (see Hebrews 13:5; Jeremiah 31:20; Ezekiel 34:11–16).

I renounce the lie that my Father God is impatient, angry, or never satisfied with what I do.

I joyfully accept the truth that my Father God is patient and slow to anger and delights in those who put their hope in His unfailing love (see Exodus 34:6; 2 Peter 3:9; Psalm 147:11).

I renounce the lie that my Father God is mean, cruel, or abusive.

I joyfully accept the truth that my Father God loves me and is gentle and protective (see Jeremiah 31:3; Isaiah 42:3; Psalm 18:2).

I renounce the lie that my Father God is trying to take all the fun out of life.

I joyfully accept the truth that my Father God is trustworthy and wants to give me a full life; His will is good, perfect, and acceptable for me (see Lamentations 3:22–23; John 10:10; Romans 12:1–2).

I renounce the lie that my Father God is controlling or manipulative.

I joyfully accept the truth that my Father God is full of grace and mercy, and gives me freedom to fail (see Hebrews 4:15–16; Luke 15:11–16).

I renounce the lie that my Father God is condemning or unforgiving.

I joyfully accept the truth that my Father God is tender-hearted and forgiving; His heart and arms are always open to me (see Psalm 130:1–4; Luke 15:17–24).

I renounce the lie that my Father God is nit-picking or a demanding perfectionist.

I joyfully accept the truth that my Father God is committed to my growth and proud of me as His growing child (see Romans 8:28–29; Hebrews 12:5–11; 2 Corinthians 7:14).

I am the apple of His eye! (Deuteronomy 32:9–10).

ON THE APP

GOD, MY FATHER

Reflect

Read through the "My Father God" truths again slowly.

Which truth strikes you the most? Why?

How do you feel as you approach *The Steps To Freedom In Christ* session (see page opposite)? Pray for each other in the light of that.

Going deeper

Invite the Holy Spirit to help you as you take a moment to consider the worst thing you have ever done. Take as long as you need to understand in your heart (not just your head) that God has completely and utterly forgiven you because of Jesus' death for you.

Ask God to show you someone you need to forgive and pledge to forgive them and anyone else you need to when you go through *The Steps To Freedom In Christ*.

In preparation for the Steps, meditate on Hebrews 12:1–2.

The Steps To Freedom In Christ

Before the next session, you will have an opportunity to do business with God using *The Steps To Freedom In Christ*.

This is an amazing opportunity for you to have time with God and take hold of your freedom from personal and spiritual issues that are holding you back. You will have time to look at where you are being deceived, uncover lies you may believe, and deal with the rubbish you have picked up in your life story.

It's not some kind of group therapy session where you all hang your dirty washing out in front of each other – you will do your business on your own with God in a quiet place.

Remember to look out for lies (false beliefs) that come to light and write them down on pages 190–191.

It really is a great opportunity. Don't miss it!

EXTRA FILM ON THE APP

INTRODUCTION TO THE STEPS TO FREEDOM IN CHRIST

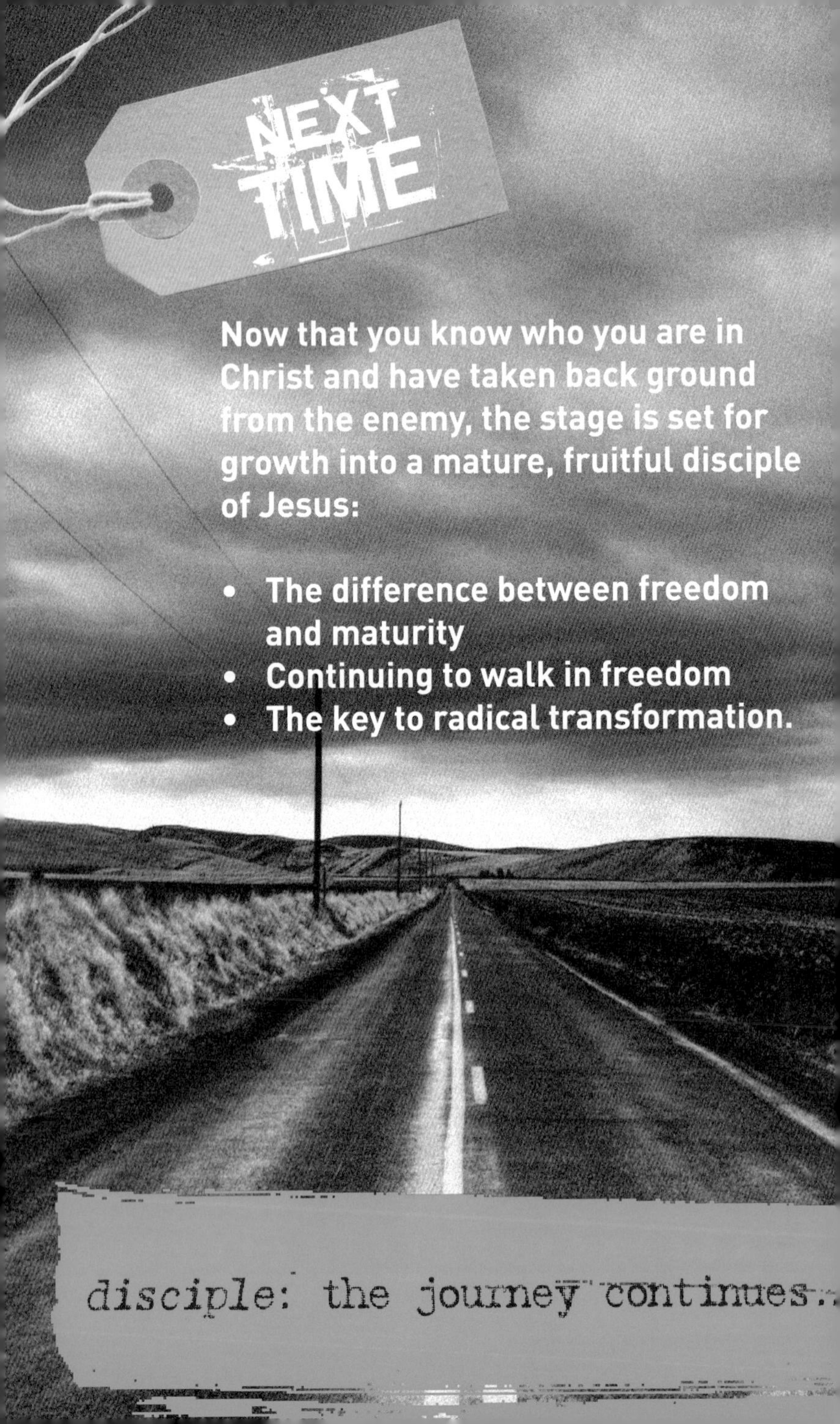
NEXT
TIME
Now that you know who you are in Christ and have taken back ground from the enemy, the stage is set for growth into a mature, fruitful disciple of Jesus:
• The difference between freedom and maturity
• Continuing to walk in freedom
• The key to radical transformation.
disciple: the journey continues...

09

Walking into the next chapter

WHY?

For though by this time you ought to be teachers, you need someone to teach you again the basic principles of the oracles of God. You need milk, not solid food, for everyone who lives on milk is unskilled in the word of righteousness, since he is a child. But solid food is for the mature, for those who have their powers of discernment trained by constant practice to distinguish good from evil.

Hebrews 5:12–14 (ESV)

Freedom is not the same thing as maturity but you can't mature until you have taken hold of your freedom. Are you now ready for solid food? If so, be prepared to make a long-term commitment to learning to distinguish good from evil, truth from lies. You can be totally transformed as you choose to renew your mind.

Declaration

In Jesus' name we declare that God is sovereign in this place and over our lives and that we are here by legal right. And so we tell every enemy of the Lord Jesus Christ to be silent and leave this place immediately. You will not stop the will of God being done in this group.

Have you become aware during the course so far of any faulty beliefs or unhelpful patterns of behaviour you have had?

How optimistic are you that you can break free from these faulty beliefs and unhelpful patterns of behaviour and genuinely change? What do you think would need to happen for you to see real transformation in these areas?

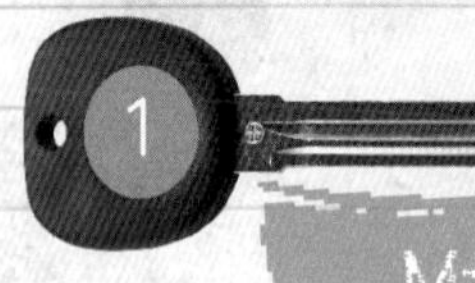

Milk or meat?

Therefore, since we are surrounded by such a great cloud of witnesses, let us throw off everything that hinders and the sin that so easily entangles. And let us run with perseverance the race marked out for us, fixing our eyes on Jesus, the pioneer and perfecter of faith.

Hebrews 12:1–2

Therefore, I urge you, brothers and sisters, in view of God's mercy, to offer your bodies as a living sacrifice, holy and pleasing to God – this is your true and proper worship. Do not conform to the pattern of this world, but be transformed by the renewing of your mind. Then you will be able to test and approve what God's will is – his good, pleasing and perfect will.

Romans 12:1–2

Christians are meant to keep growing to maturity – and there's no reason why we can't – but it's not inevitable that we will.

We will be transformed as we renew our minds.

Uncovering lies and renewing our minds with truth needs to become a regular practice. "Stronghold-busting" (see pages 141–144 and the *disciple* app) is an effective way to do this.

Stronghold:

A deeply-rooted belief that is contrary to God's Word.

THE WEAPONS WE FIGHT WITH ARE NOT THE WEAPONS OF THE WORLD. ON THE CONTRARY, THEY HAVE DIVINE POWER TO DEMOLISH STRONGHOLDS. WE DEMOLISH ARGUMENTS AND EVERY PRETENSION THAT SETS ITSELF UP AGAINST THE KNOWLEDGE OF GOD, AND WE TAKE CAPTIVE EVERY THOUGHT TO MAKE IT OBEDIENT TO CHRIST.

2 Corinthians 10:4–5

"Stronghold-Busting":
a practical way to renew your mind

1. Determine the lie you have been believing , that is to say any way you are thinking that is not in line with what God says about you in the Bible. In doing this, ignore what you feel but commit yourself wholeheartedly to God's truth.

2. Write down what effects believing the lie has had in your life. How different would your life be if you were to replace this lie with what is actually true?

3. Find as many Bible verses as you can that state the truth and write them down.

4. Write a prayer/declaration based on the formula:
   I renounce the lie that...
   I announce the truth that...

5. Finally, read the Bible verses and say the prayer/declaration out loud every day for forty days. You can set the *disciple* app to remind you each day.

Lasting change demands an intentional commitment to truth. Throughout much of this time, it will feel like you are wasting your time because the lie will *feel* true and the truth you are speaking from God's Word will *feel* unreal. However, if you persevere long enough (and it usually takes six weeks or so), your belief system *will* change and you will have been transformed through the renewing of your mind (Romans 12:2). Look at the examples on the following pages and then write your own stronghold-busters using the space on pages 146–151. Go for it!

Stronghold-Buster Example 1

Taking Comfort In Food Rather Than God

The lie: that overeating brings lasting comfort.

Effects in my life: harmful to health; becoming overweight; giving the enemy a foothold; stopping my growth to maturity

Proverbs 25:28: Like a city whose walls are broken down is a person who lacks self-control.

Galatians 5:16: So I say, walk by the Spirit, and you will not gratify the desires of the flesh.

Galatians 5:22–24: But the fruit of the Spirit is love, joy, peace, forbearance, kindness, goodness, faithfulness, gentleness and self-control. Against such things there is no law. Those who belong to Christ Jesus have crucified the flesh with its passions and desires.

2 Corinthians 1:3–4: Praise be to the God and Father of our Lord Jesus Christ, the Father of compassion and the God of all comfort, who comforts us in all our troubles, so that we can comfort those in any trouble with the comfort we ourselves receive from God.

Psalm 63:4–5: I will praise you as long as I live, and in your name I will lift up my hands. I will be fully satisfied as with the richest of foods; with singing lips my mouth will praise you.

Psalm 119:76: May your unfailing love be my comfort.

God, I renounce the lie that overeating brings lasting comfort. I announce the truth that you are the God of all comfort and that your unfailing love is my only legitimate and real comfort. I affirm that I now live by the Spirit and do not have to gratify the desires of the flesh. Whenever I feel in need of comfort, instead of turning to foods I choose to praise you and be satisfied as with the richest of foods. Fill me afresh with your Holy Spirit and live through me as I grow in self-control. Amen.

Mark off the days:

1	2	3	4	5	6	7	8	9
10	11	12	13	14	15	16	17	18
19	20	21	22	23	24	25	26	27
28	29	30	31	32	33	34	35	36
37	38	39	40					

Stronghold-Buster Example 2

Always Feeling Alone

The lie: that I am abandoned and forgotten.

Effects in my life: withdrawing from others; thinking people don't like me; seeming aloof; frightened

Deuteronomy 31:6: Be strong and courageous. Do not be afraid or terrified because of them, for the LORD your God goes with you; he will never leave you nor forsake you.

Isaiah 46:4: Even to your old age and grey hairs I am he, I am he who will sustain you. I have made you and I will carry you; I will sustain you and I will rescue you.

Jeremiah 29:11: "For I know the plans I have for you," declares the LORD, "plans to prosper you and not to harm you, plans to give you hope and a future."

Romans 8:37–38: For I am convinced that neither death nor life, neither angels nor demons, neither the present nor the future, nor any powers, neither height nor depth, nor anything else in all creation, will be able to separate us from the love of God that is in Christ Jesus our Lord.

Dear Heavenly Father

I renounce the lie that I am abandoned and forgotten and will be left on my own.

I announce the truth that you love me, that you have plans to give me a hope and a future and that absolutely nothing can separate me from your love.

In Jesus' name. Amen.

Mark off the days:

1	2	3	4	5	6	7	8	9
10	11	12	13	14	15	16	17	18
19	20	21	22	23	24	25	26	27
28	29	30	31	32	33	34	35	36
37	38	39	40					

Stronghold-Buster Example 3

Feeling Irresistibly Drawn To Internet Porn

The lie: that I cannot resist the temptation to look at internet porn.

Effects in my life: deep sense of shame; warped sexual feelings; unable to relate to other people as God intended; harmful to my marriage

Romans 6:11–14: In the same way, count yourselves dead to sin but alive to God in Christ Jesus. Therefore do not let sin reign in your mortal body so that you obey its evil desires. Do not offer the parts of your body to sin, as instruments of wickedness, but rather offer yourselves to God, as those who have been brought from death to life; and offer every part of yourself to him as an instrument of righteousness. For sin shall not be your master, because you are not under the law, but under grace.

1 Corinthians 6:19: Do you not know that your bodies are temples of the Holy Spirit?

1 Corinthians 10:13: No temptation has overtaken you except what is common to mankind. And God is faithful; he will not let you be tempted beyond what you can bear. But when you are tempted, he will also provide a way out so that you can endure it.

Galatians 5:16: So I say, live by the Spirit, and you will not gratify the desires of the flesh.

Galatians 5:22–23: But the fruit of the Spirit is love, joy, peace, forbearance, kindness, goodness, faithfulness, gentleness and self-control.

I renounce the lie that I cannot resist the temptation to look at internet porn. I declare the truth that God will always provide a way out when I am tempted and I will choose to take it. I announce the truth that if I live by the Spirit – and I choose to do that – I will not gratify the desires of the flesh and the fruit of the Spirit, including self-control, will grow in me. I count myself dead to sin and refuse to let sin reign in my body or be my master. Today and every day I give my body to God as a temple of the Holy Spirit to be used only for what honours Him. I declare that the power of sin is broken in me. I choose to submit completely to God and resist the devil who must flee from me now.

Mark off the days:

1 2 3 4 5 6 7 8 9
10 11 12 13 14 15 16 17 18
19 20 21 22 23 24 25 26 27
28 29 30 31 32 33 34 35 36
37 38 39 40

Take the biggest lie you realize you have fallen for (look at the list you have made on pages 190–191) and construct a stronghold-buster that you can use to tear it down over the next forty days or so. There is space on pages 146–147 for you to do this (and further space on the following four pages for you to put together other stronghold-busters in the future). You could also construct it in the app.

If you are struggling to think of a lie to tackle, you could pick one from this list of typical lies that Christians have come to believe:

- I am unloved
- I am a failure
- Life is hopeless
- I can never change
- God will not provide for my needs
- This will work for others but my case is special.

If you need some help to find the truth from God's Word, the "Truth Encounter" lists from Sessions 2, 3, and 8 are likely to be a good source of inspiration. If you don't have time to complete it, finish it at home.

Remember to check out the Stronghold-Buster section of the *disciple* app where you can record your stronghold-buster and set up daily reminders.

Is there someone you could encourage every day to go through their stronghold-buster?

My Stronghold-Buster 1

1. **What lie do you want to tackle?**

2. **What effect does this faulty belief have on your life? How different would your life be if you replaced it with what is actually true?**

3. **List below as many Bible verses as you can that state what God says is actually true:**

4. **Write a prayer/declaration:**

I renounce the lie that

I announce the truth that

5. **Read the Bible verses and say the prayer/declaration out loud every day for forty days. You can set the *disciple* app to remind you each day. Mark off the days below:**

1 2 3 4 5 6 7 8 9

10 11 12 13 14 15 16 17 18

19 20 21 22 23 24 25 26 27

28 29 30 31 32 33 34 35 36

37 38 39 40

My Stronghold-Buster 2

1. What lie do you want to tackle?

2. What effect does this faulty belief have on your life? How different would your life be if you replaced it with what is actually true?

3. List below as many Bible verses as you can that state what God says is actually true:

4. **Write a prayer/declaration:**

I renounce the lie that

I announce the truth that

5. **Read the Bible verses and say the prayer/declaration out loud every day for forty days. You can set the *disciple* app to remind you each day. Mark off the days below:**

1	2	3	4	5	6	7	8	9
10	11	12	13	14	15	16	17	18
19	20	21	22	23	24	25	26	27
28	29	30	31	32	33	34	35	36
37	38	39	40					

My Stronghold-Buster 3

1. What lie do you want to tackle?

2. What effect does this faulty belief have on your life? How different would your life be if you replaced it with what is actually true?

3. List below as many Bible verses as you can that state what God says is actually true:

4. **Write a prayer/declaration:**

I renounce the lie that

I announce the truth that

5. **Read the Bible verses and say the prayer/declaration out loud every day for forty days. You can set the *disciple* app to remind you each day. Mark off the days below:**

1 2 3 4 5 6 7 8 9

10 11 12 13 14 15 16 17 18

19 20 21 22 23 24 25 26 27

28 29 30 31 32 33 34 35 36

37 38 39 40

2

The goal

> Praise be to the God and Father of our Lord Jesus Christ, who has blessed us in the heavenly realms with every spiritual blessing in Christ.
>
> **Ephesians 1:3**

The goals we have developed for life may be good but if they can be blocked by others they set us up for problems;

- anxiety shows an uncertain goal
- anger shows a blocked goal
- depression can show a failed or unreachable goal

If God has a goal for your life, by definition it must be achievable. God would not ask you to do something that you couldn't do.

We can conclude that God's goal for our lives is that we become more and more like Jesus in character. He is primarily concerned with what we are *like* rather than what we *do*.

Bringing our goals into line with this will prevent a lot of anxiety, anger, and depression (but see the note on depression on page 109).

HIS DIVINE POWER HAS GIVEN US EVERYTHING WE NEED FOR A GODLY LIFE THROUGH OUR KNOWLEDGE OF HIM WHO CALLED US BY HIS OWN GLORY AND GOODNESS. THROUGH THESE HE HAS GIVEN US HIS VERY GREAT AND PRECIOUS PROMISES, SO THAT THROUGH THEM YOU MAY PARTICIPATE IN THE DIVINE NATURE, HAVING ESCAPED THE CORRUPTION IN THE WORLD CAUSED BY EVIL DESIRES.

FOR THIS VERY REASON, MAKE EVERY EFFORT TO ADD TO YOUR FAITH GOODNESS; AND TO GOODNESS, KNOWLEDGE; AND TO KNOWLEDGE, SELF-CONTROL; AND TO SELF-CONTROL, PERSEVERANCE; AND TO PERSEVERANCE, GODLINESS; AND TO GODLINESS, MUTUAL AFFECTION; AND TO MUTUAL AFFECTION, LOVE. FOR IF YOU POSSESS THESE QUALITIES IN INCREASING MEASURE, THEY WILL KEEP YOU FROM BEING INEFFECTIVE AND UNPRODUCTIVE IN YOUR KNOWLEDGE OF OUR LORD JESUS CHRIST.

2 Peter 1:3–8 (ESV)

Goals – follow the logic...

A "goal" (in the way we are using the term in this session) is something that is so important to you, that you feel your very sense of success or failure as a person depends on achieving it.

If your goal feels:

uncertain	it leads to	anxiety;
blocked	it leads to	anger;
unachievable	it leads to	depression.

But God would not ask you to do something you cannot do. So by definition no God-given goal can be uncertain, blocked, or unachievable.

Therefore, any goal that can be blocked by people or circumstances beyond your control is not a goal God wants you to have.

It may still be a good thing in itself so you don't have to abandon it. Just downgrade it from a goal to a desire. In other words don't let it determine your sense of who you are. If it doesn't happen, yes, it's a disappointment. But it's not a disaster.

Rather, adopt God's goal for your life: to become more and more like Jesus in character. Nothing and no one can block that goal – except you!

If you're honest, do you feel you're lacking something you need to become a fruitful disciple? If so,what?

Are you able to pinpoint goals that you unconsciously developed for your life, goals that you thought would make you happy or fulfilled? What were they? Why are goals that depend on the cooperation of other people or favourable circumstances unhealthy?

"God is primarily concerned with what you are like rather than what you do." What practical difference might it make in your life to realize that God's goal for you is to grow in character rather than to accomplish something specific?

Relationship not religion

> And let us consider how we may spur one another on toward love and good deeds, not giving up meeting together, as some are in the habit of doing, but encouraging one another – and all the more as you see the Day approaching.
>
> **Hebrews 10:24–25**

Although God is primarily concerned with what you are *like*, He also cares hugely about what you *do*. The big idea is that He knows that what you do will come from who you are. "The root bears the fruit" – the more like Jesus you are, the more your actions will reflect Him.

Walking with God means inviting him into our entire life.

"I alone cannot change the world but I can cast a stone that makes many ripples" – Mother Teresa

We can all leave a mark on the earth and build that treasure in heaven.

We need to be part of the body of Christ.

Reflect

Does it shock you to think that God hates religion? Ask Him to show you if any of things you do as a Christian come from a sense of religion rather than relationship.

Being a disciple is about having a real relationship with God Himself, the Creator of everything. What words would you use to describe your relationship with God right now? Tell Him your hopes and dreams for your future relationship with Him.

Are you a committed member of the Christian community? If not, ask someone to pray with you before you leave that God will show you exactly the place for you to serve and flourish.

God may still be using *disciple* to help you see areas in your belief system that are not in line with what He says is true. Continue to write them down on pages 190–191 together with the corresponding truth.

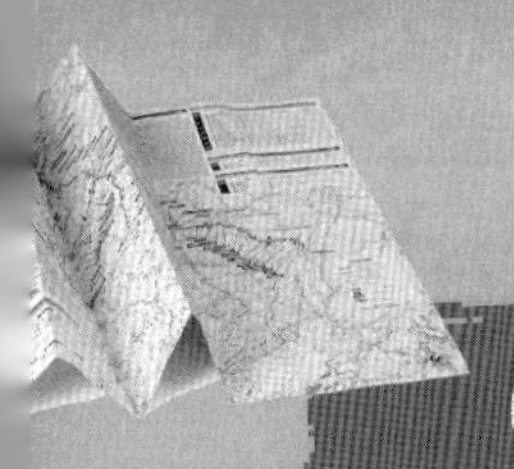

Going deeper

Take some quiet time with God on your own where you have no agenda other than seeking Him and being with Him. It might help to have some worship music and your Bible. Remember to switch off your phone and be ready to make notes of anything He may show you.

Start doing your first stronghold-buster this week and bear in mind that, in order to get to the end and see transformation in your life, it will take perseverance and effort. It will, however, be well worth it!

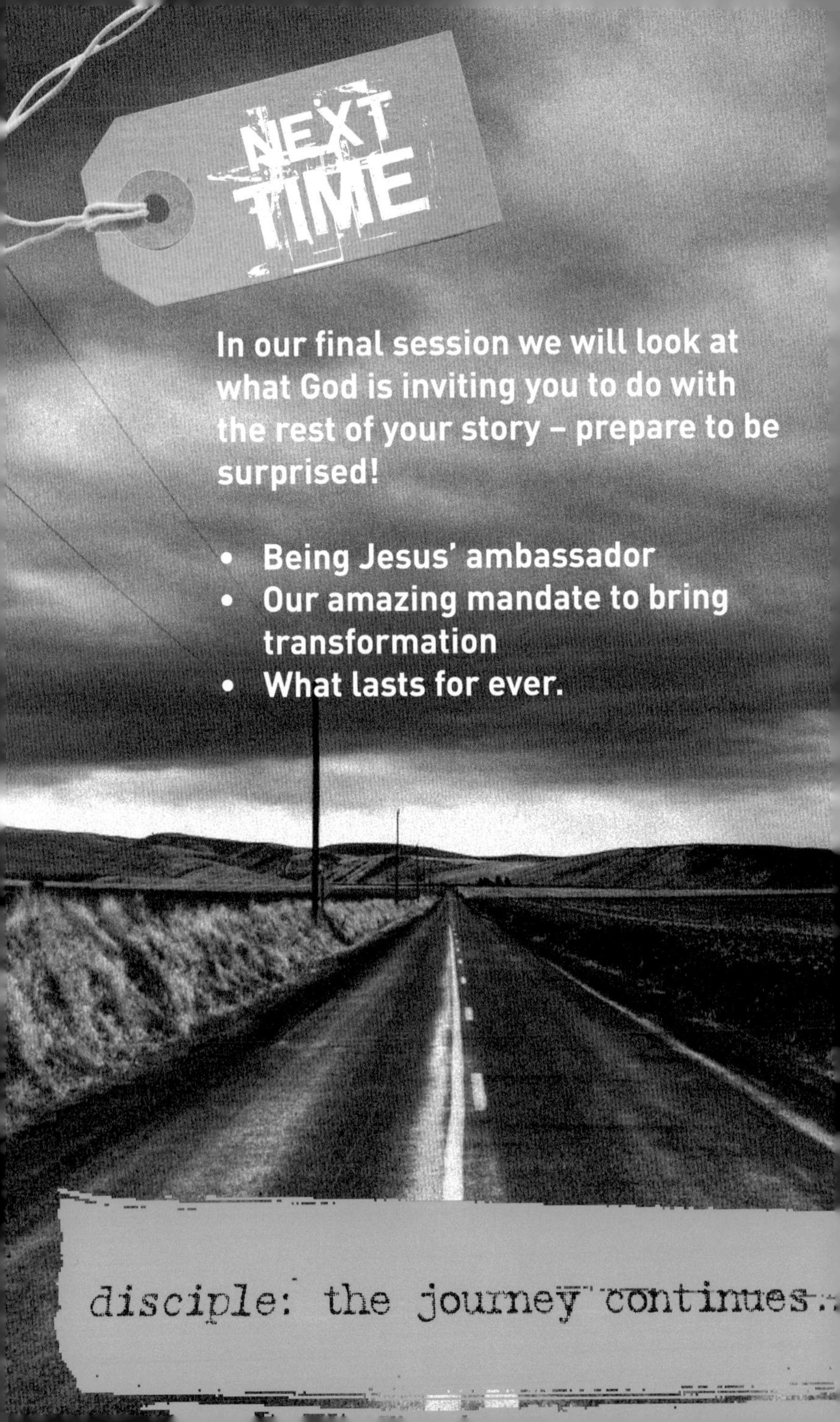
NEXT TIME
In our final session we will look at what God is inviting you to do with the rest of your story – prepare to be surprised!
• Being Jesus' ambassador
• Our amazing mandate to bring transformation
• What lasts for ever.
disciple: the journey continues...

10

Action story

WHY?

"For I know the plans I have for you," declares the Lord, "plans to prosper you and not to harm you, plans to give you hope and a future."

Jeremiah 29:11

God is God. He doesn't need us to work with Him to fulfil His incredible plan for the world. Yet He chooses to partner with us and entrust us with a staggering mandate: to bring transformation to the world around us. We are ambassadors for Christ and can choose to offer our lives to God so that we make an eternal difference.

Declaration

We declare that Jesus Christ came to destroy all of the works of the devil. The One who is in us is greater than the one who is in the world. As children of God, we declare that the devil cannot steal, kill, or destroy what God has planned to do among us today. Neither can he stop God's plans for the rest of our lives.

What is the best invitation you have ever received?

How does it make you feel to know that God invites you to join in with His work but puts you under no pressure whatsoever to do so?

God chose you and you are free to choose

> "You did not choose me, but I chose you and appointed you so that you might go and bear fruit – fruit that will last."
>
> **John 15:16**
>
> God has chosen to make known among the Gentiles the glorious riches of this mystery, which is Christ in you, the hope of glory.
>
> **Colossians 1:27**
>
> For we are God's handiwork, created in Christ Jesus to do good works, which God prepared in advance for us to do.
>
> **Ephesians 2:10**

God really did choose you! Whether you know it or not, your potential is enormous.

What you do comes from who you are.

You are in Christ:

- You are a new creation
- You are a minister of reconciliation
- You are Jesus' ambassador.

Christ is in you:

- He literally lives in you through His Spirit
- You already have everything you need to be a fruitful disciple.

THEREFORE, IF ANYONE IS IN CHRIST, THE NEW CREATION HAS COME: THE OLD HAS GONE, THE NEW IS HERE! ALL THIS IS FROM GOD, WHO RECONCILED US TO HIMSELF THROUGH CHRIST AND GAVE US THE MINISTRY OF RECONCILIATION: THAT GOD WAS RECONCILING THE WORLD TO HIMSELF IN CHRIST, NOT COUNTING PEOPLE'S SINS AGAINST THEM.

AND HE HAS COMMITTED TO US THE MESSAGE OF RECONCILIATION. WE ARE THEREFORE CHRIST'S AMBASSADORS, AS THOUGH GOD WERE MAKING HIS APPEAL THROUGH US. WE IMPLORE YOU ON CHRIST'S BEHALF: BE RECONCILED TO GOD.

GOD MADE HIM WHO HAD NO SIN TO **BE** SIN FOR US, SO THAT IN HIM WE MIGHT **BECOME** THE RIGHTEOUSNESS OF GOD.

2 Corinthians 5:17–21

PTO

If anyone builds on this foundation using gold, silver, costly stones, wood, hay or straw, his work will be shown for what it is, because the Day will bring it to light. It will be revealed with fire, and the fire will test the quality of each person's work. If what has been built survives, the builder will receive his reward. If it is burned up, the builder will suffer loss; but yet will be saved – even though only as one escaping through the flames.

1 Corinthians 3:12–15

What you do will be tested in the end – But God loves you whether you use your life to make an eternal difference or not.

There is no pressure. You have complete freedom to choose how your story goes on from here – do you want to build treasure in heaven that will last for ever or are you content with treasure on earth that is here today but will be gone tomorrow?

Think back to what you said you wanted from the rest of your life when you started *disciple* (look back at what you wrote on page 16). Has it changed at all? If so, how and why?

What difference does knowing that you are Christ's ambassador make to you?

How does the fact that Christ is in you change the way you feel about following your calling and your expectations of what might happen in your life from this point on?

2 Our incredible mandate

Always be prepared to give an answer to everyone who asks you to give the reason for the hope that you have. But do this with gentleness and respect.

1 Peter 3:15

After they prayed, the place where they were meeting was shaken. And they were all filled with the Holy Spirit and spoke the word of God boldly.

Acts 4:31

Jesus read the passage on the opposite page (see Luke 4:16–20) and finished by saying: "Today this scripture is fulfilled in your hearing." This was His mandate.

We are the Body of Christ – the actual flesh and blood through whom He works in the world. Therefore, we share Jesus' mandate to:

- proclaim the good news
- bring justice, righteousness, freedom, and transformation to our world.

Disciples of Jesus:

- Just need to be themselves
- Are prepared to give an answer
- Pray for boldness
- Live a counter-cultural existence
- Help others find true freedom.

THE SPIRIT OF THE SOVEREIGN LORD IS ON ME, BECAUSE THE LORD HAS ANOINTED ME TO PROCLAIM GOOD NEWS TO THE POOR. HE HAS SENT ME TO BIND UP THE BROKEN HEARTED, TO PROCLAIM FREEDOM FOR THE CAPTIVES AND RELEASE FROM DARKNESS FOR THE PRISONERS, TO PROCLAIM THE YEAR OF THE LORD'S FAVOUR AND THE DAY OF VENGEANCE OF OUR GOD, TO COMFORT ALL WHO MOURN, AND PROVIDE FOR THOSE WHO GRIEVE IN ZION – TO BESTOW ON THEM A CROWN OF BEAUTY INSTEAD OF ASHES, THE OIL OF JOY INSTEAD OF MOURNING, AND A GARMENT OF PRAISE INSTEAD OF A SPIRIT OF DESPAIR. THEY WILL BE CALLED OAKS OF RIGHTEOUSNESS, A PLANTING OF THE LORD FOR THE DISPLAY OF HIS SPLENDOUR.

Isaiah 61:1–3

What are some of the reasons that it can seem so hard to share about Jesus with our not-yet-Christian friends? How can we overcome our fear?

How do you feel about the truth that you are literally the flesh and blood that Jesus chooses to work through in the world? What alternative plans might God have to get His work done if we choose not to play our part (see Esther 4:14)?

Read Isaiah 61:1–3 (see previous page). If this is our mandate, what would you say are God's priorities for His people?

So, what will you choose?

> Because of the crowd he told his disciples to have a small boat ready for him, to keep the people from crowding him. For he had healed many, so that those with diseases were pushing forward to touch him.
>
> Jesus went up on a mountainside and called to him those he wanted, and they came to him. He appointed twelve that they might be with him and that he might send them out to preach and to have authority to drive out demons.
>
> **Mark 3:9–10, 13–15**

Realizing who we now are changes everything!

God is inviting us to join in with His story.

We don't have to respond to His invitation. He will love us whatever we choose. It all comes down to whether we want our lives to count for eternity, whether we want to make a real difference or not.

Will we settle for being just part of the crowd coming to Jesus for what we can get? Or, will we choose to be radical disciples, committed to fulfilling our mandate in the power of the Holy Spirit?

Reflect

What is the main thing you will take away from *disciple*?

How confident do you feel that God can use you to advance His purpose and to make a real difference that will have an eternal impact?

Pair up and pray for each other's onward journey in life as fruitful disciples who are making a difference.

Going deeper

- Ask God to show you what it means to be an ambassador for Him where He has placed you.
- Ask God to show you where there are injustices in the place He has put you and what you can do about them.

Don't forget to keep going with that stronghold-buster!

Oh... you didn't start it? No problem! Just start today. You missed a day? Don't worry – God is not cross with you! This is not some religious duty, it's a life-transforming process. Do it because you want to be different and make a difference. Just pick up where you left off and keep going until you know that you believe the truth.

EXTRA FILM ON THE APP

OVERCOMING FEAR AND TAKING A RISK FOR JESUS

A whole new beginning

So you have come to the end of *disciple*! But this is not the end of your story. In fact it's a whole new beginning, and for that reason we have given you extra pages to journal your ongoing journey from here. Do stay in touch with us through our Facebook group. We would love to see how your story is unfolding.

We hope that you have enjoyed travelling through *disciple* and that it has given you not just the inspiration and freedom to make your life count for eternity but a practical tool kit to make it happen.

We recommend that you go through *The Steps To Freedom In Christ* once a year as a kind of spiritual health check. You don't necessarily need an organized Steps day or Steps appointment. You can take each other through or even take yourself through now that the big clean-up is done!

We want to remind you that transformation does not come through trying harder or even through getting people to pray for you. It comes through renewing your mind and no one else can do that for you. It's essential that you take responsibility to continue to deal with faulty beliefs that God shows you. Keep going with those stronghold-busters even though they 'feel' pointless!

Your ongoing daily relationship with God is key. Keep talking to Him and simply enjoy being with Him with no pressure to "perform" or do anything! There is no set way to pray but we thought we would share some useful prayers (on the following pages) to start you off. Do make them your own and pray them from your heart. Remember they are not magic mantras – it's about growing in your relationship with God, not how "good" your prayers are.

Prepare to be amazed as your Heavenly Father who loves you so much unfolds more and more of His purposes for your life. What an exciting read it's going to be!

Daily prayer and declaration

Dear Heavenly Father,

Thank You that You are my Lord and Saviour and that You are in control of everything. Thank You that You're always with me and never leave me or let me go. You are the only all-powerful and wise God. You are kind and loving in every way. I love You and thank You that I am in Jesus and spiritually alive in Him. I choose today not to love the world or the world's things, and I crucify the flesh and its passions.

Thank You for the life I have in Jesus. Please fill me with the Holy Spirit so I can say no to sin and yes to You. I know that I am totally dependent on You and I take my stand against Satan and all his lies.

I choose to believe the truth of your Word not my feelings. I refuse to be discouraged; You are the God of all hope. Nothing is too difficult for You. You will meet all my needs as I choose to live by the truth of Your Word. Thank You that I can be content and live responsibly through Jesus who gives me strength.

I submit to God and take my stand against Satan and command him and all his evil spirits to leave me. I put on the whole armour of God and choose to stand firm against all the devil's schemes.

I surrender my body to You, Lord God, as a living and holy sacrifice and I choose to renew my mind by Your Word,.

I declare that I am a new creation, a holy one, a disciple of Jesus, an ambassador of Christ, and one through whom God Himself will bring righteousness, truth, and justice.

Thank You that Your plans are good, pleasing, and perfect for me.

I pray confidently as a child of God in the name of Jesus.

Amen.

Bedtime prayer

Thank You, Father God, that I am part of Your family and that You have blessed me with every spiritual blessing in Jesus.

Thank You for this time of sleep to be renewed and refreshed. I thank you for sleep as one of Your blessings for Your children and I trust You to guard my mind and my body while I am sleeping.

As I have thought about You and Your truth today, I choose to let those good thoughts stay with me while I am asleep. I trust You to protect me against every attempt of Satan and his demons to attack me while I sleep. I submit to God and command every enemy of the Lord Jesus Christ to leave my presence.

Please guard me from nightmares. I renounce all fear and cast every anxiety upon You. I specifically give you my anxieties about ____________ (list them), Father. I commit myself wholeheartedly and unreservedly to You as my rock and my fortress. Please bless this place of rest with your peace now.

I pray in the name of Jesus with confidence that You love me and have heard me. Thank you!

Amen.

Extra films

Why believe the Bible?

There are six extra films to help you look at various aspects of the course in a little more detail. Access them from the *disciple* app (see page 7).

All Scripture is God-breathed and is useful for teaching, rebuking, correcting and training in righteousness, so that the servant of God may be thoroughly equipped for every good work.

2 Timothy 3:16–17

Archaeology consistently backs up the Bible's accounts.

The Bible also proves its own contents. There are over 300 prophecies that came true about the life of Jesus alone.

Changed lives point to the truth of the Bible.

The Church keeps growing. Jesus said, "I will build my church" (Matthew 16:18) and He's been doing that ever since. There are almost certainly more Christians alive right now than have ever lived and died throughout the whole of history!

GUIDE

The gift of sex

That is why a man leaves his father and mother and is united to his wife, and they become one flesh. Adam and his wife were both naked, and they felt no shame.

Genesis 2:24–25

Do you not know that your bodies are members of Christ himself? Shall I then take the members of Christ and unite them with a prostitute? Never! Do you not know that he who unites himself with a prostitute is one with her in body? For it is said, "The two will become one flesh." But whoever is united with the Lord is one with him in spirit.

1 Corinthians 6:15–17

Part 1: As God intended

Sex is good! It was there in the Garden of Eden before sin entered the world.

The context God has created for sex is a committed relationship between a man and a woman, and specifically a marriage relationship where the commitment is affirmed before God and before other people.

Sex is not just a physical act but a spiritual act designed to bond a man and wife together. Sex outside marriage has the consequence of forming an unhelpful spiritual bond.

Being single is just as significant as being married.

No matter what your sexual history, God offers you total cleansing, forgiveness, and a brand new start.

Part 2: Pornography and masturbation

Porn and masturbation may feel like harmless fun but they can become snares that are hard to break free from. They are by nature addictive.

Porn exploits people and is essentially selfish in its expression.

Masturbation is all about self-gratification rather than an intimate union which takes account of both parties' need for intimacy. It can be hard to move from "my" needs and desires to "your" and "our" needs and desires.

Porn and masturbation can leave you open to spiritual attack and feeling ashamed and powerless.

God can set you free from any sexual bondage as you submit to Him, resist the devil, and commit to renew your mind.

The truth behind the occult

When you enter the land the Lord your God is giving you, do not learn to imitate the detestable ways of the nations there. Let no one be found among you who sacrifices their son or daughter in the fire, who practises divination or sorcery, interprets omens, engages in witchcraft, or casts spells, or who is a medium or spiritist or who consults the dead. Anyone who does these things is detestable to the Lord; because of these same detestable practices the Lord your God will drive out those nations before you.

Deuteronomy 18:9–12

Every spirit that acknowledges that Jesus Christ has come in the flesh is from God, but every spirit that does not acknowledge Jesus is not from God. This is the spirit of the antichrist.

1 John 4:2–3

The lure of the occult is to do with getting knowledge, power, healing, or peace. Of course all that can be found in God and what Satan offers are counterfeits. Nothing gives him more of a claim on you than if you dabble in the occult.

Satan cannot read your mind and does not know the future (other than what God has revealed).

The New Age movement takes spiritual practices from other religions and is at the foundation of widely accepted self-help courses, business training, and even some types of medicine. Things like guided imagery and meditation are widely accepted in workplaces, schools, and even churches. They may seem harmless but they aren't.

It is straightforward to resolve past dabbling in the occult using *The Steps To Freedom In Christ*. You submit to God by admitting that you have done it and agreeing never to do it again and then you resist the devil by claiming back the ground you gave him in your life – and he will flee, very undramatically and quietly (see James 4:7).

God, my Father

> But when the set time had fully come, God sent his Son, born of a woman, born under the law, to redeem those under the law, that we might receive adoption to sonship. Because you are his sons, God sent the Spirit of his Son into our hearts, the Spirit who calls out, "Abba, Father."
>
> **Galatians 4:4–7**

God is the source and the originator of your life. He really is your father and absolutely nothing can change that.

God loves you because He is love. (1 John 4:8).

Through your faith in Jesus Christ, you have been adopted by God. In Roman law adoption to SONSHIP meant:

- You have the right to the name and the citizenship of the person who adopted you
- You have the right to inherit their property
- You have the same rights and privileges as if you were a naturally born son.

God is interested in every aspect of your life and development (see Jeremiah 29:11). He wants you to be all that you can be and He has given you everything you need to become a growing disciple whose life will count for eternity.

As you choose to trust Him with every aspect of your life, He will guide you. Sometimes He will discipline you out of love (see Hebrews 12:6) to help you learn not to make the same mistake again.

God will never leave you or let you down (see Hebrews 13:5).

To get these truths from head to heart:

1. Make a choice not to let your past experiences define you.
2. Forgive and keep forgiving.
3. Be transformed through the renewal of your mind.

Overcoming fear and taking a risk for Jesus

God gave us a spirit not of fear but of power, love and self-control.

2 Timothy 1:7 (ESV)

There is no fear in love, but perfect love casts out fear. For fear has to do with punishment, and whoever fears has not been perfected in love.

1 John 4:18 (ESV)

The risk of not taking a risk – forty years in the wilderness for the Israelites. Joshua and Caleb were willing to risk everything because they "wholly followed the Lord." They understood their identity and by faith were willing to claim what was promised.

Fear is a gift from God designed to keep us safe. For a fear to be healthy the thing you fear needs to be present (near you) and powerful (able to do you harm). If the thing you are fearing is not near you or not able to do you harm it's an unhealthy fear.

Overcoming unhealthy fear in our lives:

1. Identify sin areas in our lives where we are choosing to yield to FEAR rather than trust and love. *The Steps To Freedom In Christ* will help you do that.
2. Acknowledge that God is always with you and that He has all power and authority.
3. Work out the lie behind the fear.
4. Counter that fear as you trust in God and choose to believe the truth. A stronghold-buster will help you replace the lie with truth.

Introduction to The Steps To Freedom In Christ

> Submit yourselves, then, to God. Resist the devil, and he will flee from you.
>
> **James 4:7**

In *disciple* we teach a way of life that, if you follow it, will lead to you making a huge impact for God. There are three elements to this way of life:

1. Understand who you really are in Christ, that you are a holy one, that God delights in you.
2. Use the power and authority you have as a child of God to take back any ground you've given to the enemy through any past mistakes.
3. Keep being transformed by the renewing of your mind as you throw out lies and choose to believe the truth.

The Steps To Freedom In Christ is a small book written by Neil Anderson that helps you put into practice the second element. It leads you through prayers concerning seven areas of your life. It is simply a tool to help you come before Jesus and ask Him to show you any issues that are holding you back and deal with them.

You are completely in control. You choose which prayers you need to pray. It's all just between you and God. If you deal with everything He shows you, you will be free. But it's not the Steps that sets you free. It's Jesus!

This is not a one-off process but a tool that you can pull out again and again whenever you need it. We recommend going through the Steps at least once a year.

Faulty Thinking (Lies)	What God Says (Truth)

Faulty Thinking (Lies)	What God Says (Truth)

Join us and equip more churches to make fruitful disciples!

A final word from Jess:

"Can you think of anything more worthwhile than helping every Christian become a fruitful disciple? At Freedom In Christ that's our passion! The impact we're seeing is breathtaking, and it's an incredibly exciting story to be part of.

"Now that you have finished *disciple*, what's next? What's your God-given mandate? There's a wealth of exciting opportunities out there to get stuck into in God's Kingdom.

"But if you're as excited as I am about the global impact of a Church truly free and fruitful, I'd love you to consider partnering with us at Freedom In Christ Ministries.

"With your regular support, we can continue to develop resources that make fruitful disciples – resources for children, youth, parents, marriages, those who are badly hurting, and those who desperately need to know who they are in Christ.

"You can help us get those resources into more churches, more communities, and more families. We can see more Christians, families, and churches all around the world firmly established in the freedom that Jesus has won for them, becoming fruitful and transforming the lives of those around them. Your regular gift can make a massive difference."

To partner with us in your country, head to:
FICMinternational.org/partner and join us in the *disciple* story.

Guide for leaders of *disciple*

An exciting new chapter!

There is something infectious about Jesus. Right from the moment He was born people came to Him in droves, from the shepherds and wise men to the crowds that swarmed about Him when He taught. He was – and remains – simply infectious.

Yet it's so easy for the millennial generation to miss Him, even those who are Christians. So many things can deflect us from a simple day-to-day relationship with Him.

Thank you for leading *disciple*. You are about to have the awesome privilege of helping young adults connect or reconnect with Jesus.

They will discover that He chooses to work through them and invites them to be part of a bigger story, a story that transcends time and promises, life, freedom, and purpose to all who choose to be part of it. It's a revolution of love, where people don't just know about Him but are transformed by Him to become true disciples who carry His presence and message into the world and make a huge difference.

The pages that follow are your guide to making your course as effective as it can possibly be. Reading them before you begin your course will significantly increase its impact.

There are three sections:

1. Understanding *disciple* – an explanation of the principles and thinking that lie behind it.
2. Leading *disciple* – practical information on preparing for and running your course.
3. Session notes – helpful information to guide you through each of the ten sessions and the ministry component.

Have fun!

Understanding *disciple*

What is disciple?

Here is a brief overview of *disciple*:

- It is a small-group discipleship course that speaks the language of the those born from the early 1980s onwards. Sociologists often refer to this generation as "the millennial generation". Churches often refer to it as "the missing generation".

- It is based on the best-selling *Freedom In Christ Course* by Neil T. Anderson and Steve Goss and will run happily alongside it.

- It contains ten sessions plus a ministry component called *The Steps To Freedom In Christ.*

- The main teaching is delivered using recorded video presented by David Edwards, Rob Peabody, and Jess Regnart but much of the learning takes place in facilitated discussions.

- An accompanying app encourages participants to engage with additional material between sessions including six shorter extra teaching sessions.

Who are the millennials?

Jess Regnart gives her perspective:
No one like labels. We don't either. Every Christian is a unique child of God and people rarely fit into neat little boxes. Yet we all have many things in common with those who were raised at the same time and in the same culture as we were. We hope you will bear with us when we use the term "the millennials" in this Leader's Guide as a shorthand way to refer to the current generation of young adults.

Sociologists have studied them, researchers have questioned them, and churches have torn their hair out over their absence. But who are they really? Rather than pigeonholing them, let's consider some common trends.

The millennials are the group of people who were born between the early 1980s and the early 2000s. They are the generation most likely to be missing in our churches. It's thought that about seven out of ten previously churched millennials have given up on faith in their transition to adulthood.

Sociologists say that this generation is marked by extreme tolerance, consumerism, narcissism, and mass consumption. Being brought up by Generation X, they have subliminally picked up the expectation that the world is their oyster so they can have whatever they want if they strive hard enough for it. "To achieve is to be" is the cultural mantra. However, they're soon hit with the reality that the world has changed since their parents "made it" in the financial boom times. It's tougher and doesn't always deliver what they feel they deserve or want regardless of how much work they do.

On the ground this may account for why so many of them seem programmed to strive, to achieve and really "be" someone. I once met a lovely student who had gone back to study in her late 20s. She was a mum but felt that she had to study to achieve, and prove herself. She hated her degree course and was struggling to balance her family life. But once she realized that her kids were the highest calling she could have, she was liberated from this heavy, heavy yoke to prove herself. I have met countless other young adults who struggle with disillusionment and a deep sense of failure when they don't get the grades/job/promotion that they wanted. This sense of failure seems to become all-consuming and devours their sense of self-worth.

Saturated in postmodernism, millennials see the notion of universal truth as a major stumbling block with many believing that everyone can have their own truth. Perhaps surprisingly, Christian millennials tend to have a fairly orthodox theology and many have a real hunger for older, more monastic rhythms. But championing orthodox theology doesn't mean that postmodernism isn't a problem to Christian millennials because the great majority feel nervous about sharing their faith. I have met so many who really want to share but just don't know how to in a culture where you can be alienated or seen as intolerant or a bigot for standing up for what you believe in. An evangelistic conversation can easily end up going round and round in circles: "Yes that's your faith and I'm pleased for you but how dare you say it's true for me."

Millennials are also the first generation actually to define themselves as consumers. They will base many decisions purely on what they get out of it. If it feels good and delivers something to them, then it must be good and the right path to follow. But if life gets tough or stops delivering, they see it as no problem simply to turn tail and try out another path or "truth". That is why all too often we see young adults make a decision to follow Jesus and get all fired up for God only to fall by the wayside and disappear when life gets tough and they don't "feel" God or don't feel their faith is "fixing" their issues. That's why real discipleship is so sorely needed.

And finally, in contrast to their parents, millennials don't give much credence to institutions or even trust them to do the right thing. When you understand this aspect, it becomes a little less surprising that so many struggle with having faith in God. After all, He is seen as being represented by an institution – the Church – which says He is the only truth and some of whose followers come across as bigoted and intolerant.

So what does it look like out there in the world? Well, as you would expect from any generation where so few know God in any capacity, and where those who do know Him are ill-equipped or feel unable to share, this is a generation in crisis. Having attended two academic establishments in the last five years and having had the privilege of shadowing mental health services, I can testify that self-harming and eating disorders are at an epidemic level. University and college counselling services are overrun with students struggling with anxiety and depression. Casual sex, binge drinking, drug abuse, porn addiction, gambling, and the occult are not only on the rise but in some cases even socially desirable.

And yet this is a generation with huge potential and God has plans for them! Millennials tend to be resourceful and entrepreneurial. They are motivated self-starters. They are concerned with social justice and many want to make a real difference in their working lives. They are also hugely generous, with 47 per cent of Christian millennials tithing their income. Being super-connected through social media, many become role models to their peers and have much to teach the generations that have come before them.

They are also hugely hungry for authenticity and spirituality. Whilst they may dislike what they can perceive as hypocrisy in the Church, and many don't attend a church because they don't like the way it's run, they are hungry for a relationship with God and are very open to Him when they see Him as he really is: a loving God with a gospel of grace rather than a gospel of rules.

Millennials are hungry for role models who are authentic and real. They are looking for people who live by what they believe, who communicate in a relevant and accessible way, who don't patronize them or tell them what to believe but wrestle with issues and questions alongside them. It's a sad reality that 33 per cent of Christian millennials say that they have no mentor or friends that they can debate with and be accountable to and 50 per cent feel that they are not being equipped or taught to live out their faith at work.

They are crying out for role models and mentors but many Christian millennials feel that older Christians struggle to relate to them so communication is a key issue. Leaders of millennials would do well to realize that, far from being impossible to communicate with or teach, they simply communicate and learn in a different way. It's not a worse or substandard way, it's just different. A millennial is less likely to spend hours reading every book that was ever written on a subject and is far more likely to listen to a podcast, read an online blog, or watch an internet clip. And if they want to share something with the world they will post it on social media, debate it online, and even make their own online clip that might reach hundreds of people in one go.

This is a generation that knows how to access information quickly, how to promote a cause they believe in, and how to be heard by the world. This is a generation of people who already have so much in place to lead their peers.

Whilst they tend to turn away from what they perceive as organized religion and a list of dos and don'ts, when millennials come to faith, they really encounter God. They follow Jesus with a freshness, determination, and passion which is nothing short of beautiful and astounding. An amazing 89 per cent of Christian millennials attend church weekly with some 84 per cent of them serving in church for the benefit of others.

Far from being a difficult and rebellious generation, Christian millennials are an amazing group of people; gifted, talented, and chosen by God. They are the new wine, very different from previous generations but with much to teach those who have come before them. The millennials are the leaders of tomorrow with amazing potential to fulfil the amazing plans that God has for them.

The statistics quoted are mostly taken from research by the Evangelical Alliance that you can find here: www.eauk.org/church/one-people-commission/together-we-can-build-tomorrows-church.cfm

Understanding the approach of disciple

What do you understand by the term "disciple"? Historically the Church has seen discipleship essentially as teaching Christians what to *do* now that they have turned to Christ. It has, for example, taught them about the importance of daily devotions, the sacraments, baptism, worship, and so on. There is, of course, an important place for all of those things but that in our view is not what discipleship is about.

In fact if people get the impression that discipleship or growing as a Christian is all about "learning to behave in the right way" it tends to lead to joyless legalism where they try their best to perform well, to live up to expectations. They end up labouring under a constant sense that they are letting God down or else under the delusion that they are "doing it right" which makes them proud and Pharisaical.

In the Bible, the goal of discipleship is not getting people to behave outwardly in a certain way. It's about inner transformation. The fruit of the Spirit in Galatians 5 – love, joy, peace, etc. – is all about character qualities. God is not primarily concerned with what you *do* but what you are *like*. Because what you do will flow from what you are like – and you'll do those acts of love and sacrifice not because you feel you have to but because you want to, out of love for Jesus.

Our definition of a disciple is someone who is "learning to become more and more like Jesus in character". As that happens, they will increasingly act like Him too.

There are three key principles at the heart of *disciple*.

1. Know who you are in Christ

The most critical thing in helping people become a fruitful disciple is that they understand exactly what happened the moment they turned to Christ. In our experience at least 90 per cent of Christians don't understand that they have become someone completely new.

This explains why simply teaching people how to behave does not work. Take any one of Paul's letters to the churches and see how far you read before you get to any kind of instruction on how to behave. I'll save you the trouble – it's always at least halfway through. Yet, of course, he is concerned that the Christians he is writing to behave like Christ. Why doesn't he come straight out with it and tell them what to do? Because he knows that will lead to legalism – "trying harder".

So what does he do in the first half of the letter? He focuses on helping Christians understand just who they are now that they are in Christ and what they have in Christ. In his great prayer in Ephesians 1:18–19, for example, he prays that the eyes of the Ephesians' hearts will be opened so that they understand just who they are and what they have in Christ. When they know these things, the rest simply follows: people live for Him not because they feel they have to but because they know Him and love Him. And they know that He loves and accepts them.

Paul explains that at one time, "we were by nature deserving of wrath" (Ephesians 2:3). In other words, no matter how good our outward behaviour, deep down inside we were offensive to God and we couldn't do anything about it.

The moment you became a Christian was the defining moment of your life. Everything changed for you. The language he uses is very dramatic:

"If anyone is in Christ, he is a new creation. The old has passed away; behold, the new has come." (2 Corinthians 5:17, ESV) According to that verse, can you be partly old creation and partly new? No! It's like those offers you sometimes see in supermarkets where they say, "When it's gone, it's gone." The old has gone. It's akin to a caterpillar changing into a butterfly. You're either a caterpillar or a butterfly, not half and half.

"For you were once darkness, but now you are light in the Lord." (Ephesians 5:8) Can you be both light and darkness? Not according to that verse.

"He has rescued us from the dominion of darkness and brought us into the kingdom of the Son he loves." (Colossians 1:13) Can you still be in both kingdoms? No.

Many Christians have come to think of themselves as "a sinner saved by grace". They know they are forgiven but not much else is different.

Here's an interesting verse: "While we *were* still sinners, Christ died for us" (Romans 5:8). It seems to imply that we are no longer sinners.

You certainly were a sinner, and you were saved by grace alone. So if you're no longer a sinner who or what are you?

In the New Testament, it is unbelievers who are consistently identified as "sinners". Believers on the other hand are consistently identified as "holy ones" or, to use the traditional translation, "saints" – and never clearly the other way round. If you have received Jesus as your Lord, you are not a forgiven sinner but a redeemed saint! Our very nature – who we are deep down inside – has been transformed from an object of wrath into someone who shares God's own nature (see 2 Peter 1:4). We have been changed from being someone who could not help but displease God to someone who is accepted, secure, and significant in Christ.

Even when we go wrong and fall into sin – which we do – our primary identity as a holy one remains intact.

Consider two pictures from the parable that Jesus told in Luke 15 that is traditionally referred to as "the parable of the prodigal son":

First the younger son at the point that he collapses into his father's arms and casts himself on his mercy. He can scarcely believe his father's grace as he realizes that, even though he richly deserves it, he will not be punished. He realizes that he is forgiven and accepted but he also knows that he is dirty, smelly, and broken. He is acutely aware of his failure and deeply ashamed of what he has become. This is how many Christians see themselves. Forgiven but still essentially the same no good rotten people they always were.

It's as if our understanding of the Gospel has got as far as Good Friday: Jesus died for my sins and I'm going to go to Heaven when I die. But nothing much changes right now.

But the Father does not leave the son there. Here's the second picture. It's the same son just a matter of minutes later. Now, he is wearing the best robe in the house, symbolizing that he had once again been given the right to enjoy the place of "right standing" with the Father, that he was completely restored. He has been given back the signet ring that was used on official documents and could be instantly recognizable as the Father's mark. In other words, this boy, who had squandered his father's wealth in wild living, has been given the authority to spend money again. And he is wearing sandals. In a Jewish household, the only people allowed to wear footwear in the house were the father and his sons, so the father is declaring in no uncertain terms that the boy, despite everything he had done, is still his son, entitled to the rights of a son.

Which picture most accurately represents how you see yourself in relation to God? In our experience most Christians get stuck on the first picture, knowing we're forgiven but still feeling we are miserable sinners.

We need to encourage people to move on to the second picture. We need to make it through to Easter Sunday and realize that it's not just about Jesus rising from the dead. *We* rose from the dead too and became someone completely new; we need to know that we are now holy ones, saints, that we share God's very nature.

In order to be free to be motivated by love, we have to know that we are more than just forgiven. Now that the younger son, knowing that he deserved nothing but punishment, has been completely restored, how do you think he will behave from this point onwards? Won't he want to work for the father simply because he is loved rather than because he has to or because he's working for a reward? When you know who you are in Christ, the good works follow naturally, coming from a heart relationship with the father rather than any sense of religious duty.

2. See reality as God says it is

Sometimes people have the impression that faith is all about summoning up some superhuman strength so that you can believe something that isn't really true in the hope of making it true. Faith is actually the opposite of that. It is making a choice to believe what is already true. God has set the world up in a specific way, what you might call "the way things are" or "how it is", and has chosen to reveal how it works in the Bible. If we act in accordance with how God says it is, then our lives will work. We'll grow in character and He will be able to use us.

Walking by faith boils down to finding out from God's Word what is already true and making a choice to believe it. In other words one of our key roles as leaders of *disciple* is to help people see reality the way God says it actually is.

The problem is that all of us naturally have a warped view of the world. We look at it through filters or lenses – but we don't realize that. These filters can be based on our past experiences. Often they come from the way we have learned to look at the world that comes from the culture we live in – our worldview.

In an East African country, an evangelical missionary organization was ready to hand over leadership of the church they had planted to African leaders. Two men were presented for the position. One of them went to a witch doctor to secure a charm to enhance his chances of being chosen as leader of the church. What was this man saying about what he really believed? He was saying, "I'm not sure about the power of God, but I really believe in the power of the witch doctor." That may sound ridiculous to those of us brought up in the West but he was simply reverting to his core beliefs, his worldview, how he had come to believe the world functions. That outweighed his Christian beliefs even though those were really true. His worldview deceived him and led him into sin.

It's just the same for those of us who have been brought up in the West. We think that we see the world as it is but the Western worldview predisposes us to look at it in a certain way. In particular it denies the reality of the spiritual world. So, although we and our people will recognize the existence of Satan and demons theologically and intellectually, we are predisposed to run our lives and our ministries as if they aren't there.

So one of the things we need to do is to help people understand that we are up against an unseen enemy. We need to explain how the spiritual world works because it's a necessary step to understanding that in Christ you do not ever need to let the enemy get the better of you. This is not to frighten people – in fact quite the opposite – it's to help them understand that they are the ones seated with Christ in the heavenly realms far above all power and authority. And also to help them realize that it's possible for Christians unwittingly to let the enemy influence them – but also very easy to take that ground back.

Some might say, "Do you mean there might be demons around me?" Well, the spiritual world is filled with demons, but so what? You have no reason to be frightened about that. What else is around you that you can't see but which has the potential to do you a lot of harm? Germs!

What is an appropriate response to the fact that there are germs all around? Put on a protective suit and spray disinfectant all over the place? No! The proper response is to live a balanced life of rest, exercise, and diet – eat enough fruit and vegetables, get enough sleep, and then simply let your immune system protect you.

What's an appropriate response to the fact that there are demons all around? Simply to fix our eyes on Jesus and live a righteous life by faith in the power of the Holy Spirit. We certainly don't need to go looking for them behind every bush.

The danger comes for those Christians who don't realize that demons are there and don't understand the way they work and how to protect themselves. When doctors didn't know there were germs, they didn't sterilize their instruments or scrub their hands and people died. Christians who don't know about the reality of the spiritual world don't see any need to put on the armour of God and "take captive every thought to make it obedient to Christ" (2 Corinthians 10:5). That makes it easy for the enemy to neutralize them.

So a crucial aspect of discipleship is teaching people how God says the world works. He says clearly that if we let the sun go down on our anger and let it turn into sin, we give the enemy a foothold (Ephesians 4:26–27). That unresolved sin will short circuit God's power to enable us to live righteously. It makes it difficult to resist further temptation – difficult to make the right choice. And the more you seem unable to get out of the cycle, the more the enemy accuses you and the more shame you feel. At this point so many give up and walk away.

Just sinning and confessing, sinning and confessing, doesn't do it. Why? Because that's not complete repentance. James 4:7 says, "Submit yourselves, then, to God. Resist the devil, and he will flee from you." When we confess, that's just the first bit – the submitting. We need to go on and complete our responsibility by actively resisting the devil and taking back the foothold that we've given to the enemy that allows sin to reign in our body.

Most Christians have simply not been taught how to do this. But it's actually quite straightforward. There is a ministry process to help people do it in *disciple* that comes between Sessions 8 and 9. It's called *The Steps to Freedom in Christ* and it's a great process to go through once a year as a kind of spiritual check-up. It's a crucial part of helping people understand reality and the choices they can make to take hold of their freedom and keep walking in that freedom.

Once you've removed any footholds, focus on Jesus. Live a righteous life in the power of the Holy Spirit.

3. Renew your mind

We have seen that deep down inside we have already been transformed – we have become wholly new people. But an ongoing transformation of character also needs to take place so that we become more and more like Jesus.

A key question: how can Christians be transformed?

Trying harder? Being prayed for? Being filled with the Holy Spirit? Don't misunderstand us – those are good things. But the New Testament is clear. Romans 12:2 says that we are transformed through the renewing of our minds.

The spiritual battle that we are in plays out in our minds. It's a battle for truth. It's as we commit ourselves wholeheartedly to believe what is true and throw out old ways of thinking based on lies, that we are changed to become more and more like Jesus who is the Truth.

Some of your participants may instinctively want you or God to do that for them but in the way God has set the world up, whose responsibility is it? The individual disciple's. We have to teach them to do it. It can seem like bad news to them that they have to do it but actually it is great news because it means that the key to transformation is in their own hands. As they get hold of this the effects are astonishing.

A key truth for growing disciples to understand is that they are in charge of their mind. They are like air traffic controllers with lots of different planes (thoughts) asking for permission to come in to land. They can decide which thoughts to allow to land and which to send away.

All of us have a different family background, different past experiences, and differing worldviews. We have all unconsciously developed a set of beliefs – default behaviour if you like. We may not really be aware of them but they are there. And many of them do not agree with God's Word. The ongoing process of maturing as a Christian is all about uncovering our faulty beliefs and replacing them with what is really true.

disciple, therefore, puts a lot of emphasis on truth and lies. Jesus said that it's knowing the truth that sets you free (John 8:32). But that doesn't mean just a head knowledge where we give intellectual assent but don't apply it. Before we can be said really to *know* the truth, we need to have taken hold of it in our hearts. But that journey from head to heart can be a very long one.

In *disciple* we help people work out where their belief system is not in line with truth and in Session 9 we teach a very practical way of renewing the mind that we call "Stronghold-Busting" that works amazingly well if participants will persevere to the end of the process.

Conclusion

A common refrain we hear from participants on Freedom In Christ's discipleship courses is, "I wish that someone had told me this thirty years ago." The reality is that very many Christians don't understand who they are and what they have now that they are in Christ; they struggle to see reality in the way God says it is; and they are expecting either God or some Christian who is more spiritual or anointed than they are to say the right words over them so that they can be transformed when all along the key is in their own hands. *disciple* is an exciting opportunity to help millennial Christians take hold of these truths much earlier in their lives than they might otherwise do.

As we help them to do that and encourage them to put them into practice, we will see transformation. They will become more and more like Jesus – which is the true goal of discipleship – and will therefore behave more and more like Jesus.

As individual lives are transformed, churches will be transformed. They will then go on to transform communities. There is no limit to what the Body of Christ can do as we work in unity in the power of the Holy Spirit.

And *disciple* is designed to help you play your part as you lead others on that journey.

Where does *disciple* fit with other Freedom In Christ resources?

Different people think in different ways. We are all affected by the worldview we grew up with much more than we usually imagine. We all have different "programming". What communicates well to one person or to one group will not make the same sense to another. That's why we constantly have to adapt how we present the great truths of God's Word. The Apostle Paul knew all about this:

> I have made myself a slave to everyone, to win as many as possible. To the Jews I became like a Jew, to win the Jews. To those under the law I became like one under the law (though I myself am not under the law), so as to win those under the law. To those not having the law I became like one not having the law (though I am not free from God's law but am under Christ's law), so as to win those not having the law. To the weak I became weak, to win the weak. I have become all things to all people so that by all possible means I might save some. I do all this for the sake of the gospel, that I may share in its blessings. (1 Corinthians 9:19–23)

It's always been necessary to present God's unchanging truth in new ways because experiences, priorities, and understanding constantly change.

This is especially true as one generation succeeds another. What worked ten years ago doesn't work so well now. It's not that the truth has changed or that people and their needs are fundamentally different, it's just that every generation sees the world differently and connects with God's truth differently. The advent of the internet and electronic gadgets has speeded this process up: those born as "internet natives" process information quite differently to those who were not.

In recent years young adults throughout the Western world have turned their back on the Church (though not necessarily on Jesus) in large numbers. Church leaders are crying out for a way to stop that happening. They don't connect well with the language and style of an older generation. They need to hear the crucial truths of the gospel in their own language. And that's what *disciple* is about.

Freedom In Christ Ministries aims to equip the Church around the world to make disciples of Jesus who are genuinely fruitful. Our strategy is to create excellent resources, put them into the hands of leaders, and then do everything we can to assist those leaders as they use them.

The main strategic resource worldwide is *The Freedom In Christ Course* by Neil T. Anderson and Steve Goss which has been translated into around thirty languages and used by hundreds of thousands of people. It is regularly updated and is the main tool for churches that are using the Freedom In Christ approach to discipleship.

Alongside *The Freedom In Christ Course* stand a number of other resources that are based on the same principles but are in some way more specialized. *The Grace Course* helps people take some of the key principles deeper. *Freed To Lead* helps people apply the principles to leadership. *Freedom In Christ For Young People* presents the principles in a way that communicates to teens. There are other resources for other areas and, of course, many excellent books by Neil T. Anderson and others that course participants and church leaders alike will find extremely helpful.

So where does *disciple* fit in? *disciple* takes the teaching principles from *The Freedom In Christ Course* and presents them in a way that communicates to the millennial generation – those born from the early 1980s onwards.

Of course, many millennials have hugely appreciated *The Freedom In Christ Course* and been transformed as they have done business with God through it. We're equally certain that many who were born before the early 1980s will also appreciate *disciple*. However, generally speaking, people will find the message speaks more directly to them – and is therefore more effective – if they are using the resource that communicates most effectively to their generation.

Like Paul we want to "become all things to all people", to do everything we possibly can to communicate the message in the way that best helps people receive it.

Our recommendation, therefore, is that most people in a typical church will get the most benefit from *The Freedom In Christ Course* and that this should be the main discipleship tool. Use this if your audience is primarily over the age of 35 or covers a broad range.

However, *disciple* fits very happily alongside it as a resource for the millennial generation. Use this if your audience is mostly composed of people in their 20s and 30s.

Freedom In Christ For Young People fits alongside both and effectively helps teens connect with the truth.

Each resource contains the same unchanging truths communicated in a way that speaks clearly to its intended audience.

Leading disciple

How it works

disciple is fun, interactive, and easy to lead. It covers the topics that matter to millennials. It's packed with key truths and honest, sometimes raw stories. It has ten sessions plus a ministry component that comes between Sessions 8 and 9.

This Leader's Guide provides all the information you need to take others on this journey, step by step, chapter by chapter. We've kept it concise.

Each session kicks off with a short Starter Film which raises some relevant questions. Then the main teaching is split into three further short films each followed by opportunities to respond in small discussion groups. That's because a key characteristic of millennials is that they like to discuss things and make their own decisions rather than be spoon-fed information and expected to "just believe it".

In addition there are encouragements to participants to go deeper by wrestling with the concepts between sessions. The *disciple* app, for example, will send them a small nugget of teaching or question to consider every day. The app also includes additional teaching films on extra topics that are important – they may be surprised at how relevant the content is to them.

Course components:

disciple Leader's Guide

ISBN: 978-0-85721-698-4

We recommend that, if possible, everyone leading a group has their own copy of this Leader's Guide which also incorporates the content of the Participant's Guide (below). It contains essential information on leading the course – particularly on leading the discussion times. Note that although it includes a precis of the teaching for each session, it does not include the entire script as the main teaching is designed to be delivered using the DVDs.

disciple DVD Set

ISBN: 978-0-85721-700-4

Contains the main teaching for each of the ten sessions. The DVDs pause automatically for the Starter Film and Chat discussion times. Press play to continue when your group is ready. The DVD has optional subtitles in English for those who are hearing-impaired and as an aid for those whose first language is not English.

disciple Participant's Guide

ISBN: 978 0 85721 701 1 Pack of 5: 978 0 85721 702 8

Each participant will need a copy of the Participant's Guide which contains comprehensive notes for each session and the Chat and Reflect times. As well as enabling participants to follow the teaching, there is plenty of extra info to help people engage with the sessions and space to journal.

The Steps To Freedom In Christ

For the ministry component of *disciple*, every participant will need a copy of *The Steps To Freedom In Christ* booklet by Neil Anderson. The booklet is published in different formats in different countries. Consult the website of your local Freedom In Christ office to find the appropriate version for you.

The Steps To Freedom In Christ DVD

A DVD that guides people through the process is available if you prefer not to lead the process yourself. We recommend this for groups because it frees leaders up to be available to participants rather than concentrating on the mechanics of the process. Consult the website of your local Freedom In Christ office to find the appropriate version for your country.

disciple App

Participants are strongly encouraged to download the *disciple* app. It gives access to six additional shorter teaching sessions that they can go through on their own, the "Truth Encounter" lists from Sessions 2, 3, and 8, and the Starter Film for each session. In addition it will help them develop and use a "Stronghold-Buster" to renew their mind. It also provides a daily devotional based on the principles in *disciple*. The material for the first few sessions is freely available. The rest can be unlocked for a small payment.

Truth Encounter Postcards

Sessions 2, 3, and 8 each contain a key list of Biblical truth that we call "Truth Encounter" lists. They are printed in the Participant's Guide and are available on the *disciple* app but participants will also appreciate having these postcards, one for each list. They are great for popping into a Bible or pinning to a wall as a reminder of the amazing truth they will learn as they go through the course.

disciple Invitations

We have produced packs of invitations you can use to promote the course. They contain the basic course details with space for you to add your own information using a printer or copier.

Poster

There is a *disciple* poster available with space for you to add brief details of your course.

Consult the website of your country's Freedom In Christ Ministries office (see page 352) to order the items you need.

What's in each session?

Each of the ten teaching sessions is structured in the same way and contains several common components.

Welcome

Each session begins with a time that we describe as "Welcome" (though it is not labelled as such in the Participant's Guide). It's a time to help people settle in and feel comfortable so we suggest having coffee, tea, and pastries available. It's also a time to set the scene for the main input. Keep a careful eye on the time to ensure that the Welcome does not overrun.

We suggest that your Welcome includes the following elements:

Brief Introduction

The "Why?" page at the start of each session in the Participant's Guide together with the "Next Time" page at the end of the previous session (or for Session 1, "The Start" on page 10) gives participants a flavour of what the session will cover. You may like to have someone read them out or summarize them in your own words.

Short Time Of Worship

Worship centres our lives on God and welcomes the Holy Spirit to protect and lead the course. We do not suggest any particular means or form of worship. Just do what is appropriate in your context.

Prayer

This is a spiritual exercise not just an intellectual one, so inviting God through prayer to take an active role in the session is essential. In the Leader's Notes for each session you will find a suggested prayer but, of course, you can also use your own.

Declaration

Satan wants to distract and disrupt. Speaking out a declaration is a great way to remind him that he has no power to stop the will of God being done in the session (and we can be confident that making disciples is the will of God!). From Session 6 onwards we encourage participants to join in with a declaration at the start of each session. Encourage people to do this confidently and boldly because they are children of God seated with Christ in the heavenly realms far above the devil!

Starter Film

The Starter Film is a short impactful film shot on location with a couple of open questions for discussion. Hopefully participants will have watched it already via the app but show it again now. It is designed simply to set the scene and stimulate discussion and openness in your group. Don't feel the need to do any teaching during this time – the most important thing is that people talk.

Keys

The three Keys sections of each session with their integrated Chat and Reflect questions, form the heart of the *disciple* teaching content. Participants will watch them on the DVD.

Each section is presented by a different person and typically lasts nine or ten minutes. At the end of each Keys section, the DVD will pause automatically for a response to what has been taught.

After Key 1 and Key 2, the response takes the form of Chat questions. These are usually questions for group discussion and we would suggest breaking people down into groups of four or five people for these. Much of the learning will take place in these times.

After Key 3, the response time is called Reflect and is designed to be a quieter, more reflective, prayerful time where participants will begin to do business with God. We would suggest breaking people down into twos or threes for these or sometimes letting people have time with God on their own (the leader's notes for each session will give guidance on this). You might even consider keeping the whole group together and leading the time of quiet reflection yourself.

During this time (and indeed at any other appropriate point during the sessions) refer people to the "Faulty Thinking Versus What God Says" section on pages 190–191. A hugely important part of *disciple* is helping people work out where their belief system is out of line with what God says is true and giving them a tool called "Stronghold-Busting" to help them renew their minds (this is explained in Session 9). We want participants to get into the habit of making a note on these pages of any "lie" they come to realize they have been believing, together with the corresponding truths from the Bible. They can then use these pages to decide which areas of faulty thinking they want to address once they come to Session 9.

Sessions 2, 3, and 8 each feature a "Truth Encounter" list of Biblical truth. These can be extremely powerful if participants take the time to read them out day by day.

Going Deeper
Each session concludes with a "Going Deeper" component which is designed to help participants continue to grapple with the concepts learned during the following week.

So, at the end of each session, draw people's attention to it and encourage them to consider the questions day by day. As you do this, take care not to lapse into legalism! In other words, please be clear that this is entirely optional – we want people to do it because they want to grow as disciples and make their lives count, not in order to please you or because they feel they have to.

This is a good place to remind people to use the app between sessions to watch the Starter Film for the following week, access the extra films, read out the "Truth Encounter" lists or work on their Stronghold-Busters.

How long per session?

Here is a suggested range of timings for a typical session:

Welcome	**20–30 minutes**

This would be broken down approximately as follows:

Getting drinks etc.	2–3 minutes
Prayer, declaration, and worship	5–9 minutes
Starter Film	3 –5 minutes
Discussion	10–15 minutes

Keys	**60–90 minutes**

Keys 1 – 3 (on DVD)	25–30 minutes
Chat 1	10–20 minutes
Chat 2	10–20 minutes
Reflect	10–20 minutes

The total length of the video for the Keys section of each session is around 25–30 minutes. See the following page for detailed timings.

If you used the maximum time for each segment, your session would last 120 minutes. If you used the minimum time, it would last 80 minutes. We suggest that you plan your sessions to last no more than 120 minutes and, in our experience, 90 minutes is usually the optimum. Tailor your timings accordingly.

It is especially important to keep a careful eye on how long Welcome takes, because this is the area where most groups overrun consistently. Reflect is important, so it is better to plan a shorter time for the opening components to ensure that you do not take time away from the end.

Detailed Timings For The DVDs

To help you plan the length of each filmed segment is shown below (in minutes and seconds). The DVD pauses automatically between segments.

Session 1		**Session 2**	
Starter Film:	4:07	Starter Film:	3:36
Key 1:	13:32	Key 1:	8:33
Key 2:	8:46	Key 2:	7:29
Key 3:	6:05	Key 3:	13:30
TOTAL:	32:30	TOTAL:	33:08
Session 3		**Session 4**	
Starter Film:	3:00	Starter Film:	4:37
Key 1:	4:02	Key 1:	13:11
Key 2:	8:43	Key 2:	5:36
Key 3:	15:02	Key 3:	8:59
TOTAL:	30:47	TOTAL:	32:23
Session 5		**Session 6**	
Starter Film:	3:37	Starter Film:	3:52
Key 1:	7:14	Key 1:	9:38
Key 2:	6:46	Key 2:	8:57
Key 3:	9:49	Key 3:	6:28
TOTAL:	27:26	TOTAL:	28:55
Session 7		**Session 8**	
Starter Film:	2:56	Starter Film:	5:06
Key 1:	6:36	Key 1:	8:40
Key 2:	11:36	Key 2:	6:41
Key 3:	8:44	Key 3:	14:04
TOTAL:	29:52	TOTAL:	34:31
Session 9		**Session 10**	
Starter Film:	4:42	Starter Film:	3:55
Key 1:	12:00	Key 1:	8:40
Key 2:	9:56	Key 2:	11:43
Key 3:	7:54	Key 3:	8:51
TOTAL:	34:32	TOTAL:	33:09

How does the ministry component work?

Participants are given the opportunity to go through *The Steps To Freedom In Christ* between Sessions 8 and 9. It's a gentle, kind, undramatic process but it can make an enormous difference. Many Christians rank it second in importance only to their conversion experience. Please don't be tempted to overlook it. To do so would significantly lessen the impact of *disciple*.

There is much more information on the process in the Steps To Freedom In Christ section of this Leader's Guide (starting on page 311) but it's important to work out as early as possible how you will approach it and plan accordingly. There are two different approaches you can use:

1. An individual "freedom appointment"

This is the ideal. In this scenario each individual is led through the process by an "encourager", with a prayer partner in attendance, in a session that typically lasts three to six hours. It can be amazingly upbuilding when people in a church or small group are willing to confess their sins to one another and pray for each other (see James 5:16). Encouragers and prayer partners do not generally need any special skills other than a reasonable maturity in Christ and an understanding of the Biblical principles of freedom, but will benefit from having attended a Helping Others Find Freedom In Christ course (either live or on DVD) or having read *Discipleship Counseling* by Neil Anderson (Regal Books, 2003).

2. As a group on an "away day"

Taking your group away for a day (or even a weekend) to go through the Steps works well. It allows everyone to go through the Steps at the same time whilst ensuring that people have enough time to do business with any issues that the Holy Spirit brings to their mind. This is the option that most people choose.

It is best to book a location away from your church and to include times of worship. You will need leaders to make themselves available to participants who may need help at various times.

You can also include one or more of the normal sessions in this time if it suits you. It works particularly well to include Session 8 (Forgiving From The Heart) in the away day directly before the forgiveness step. If you go away for a longer time, you could also cover Sessions 9 and 10 so that the away day forms the conclusion to the whole course.

We would suggest that your group is given the relevant dates for their diary as soon as possible, ideally at the time they sign up for *disciple*, and that you consistently make clear that this is an essential part of the course and not to be missed.

Preparing to lead

You don't need to be theologically trained or a church leader to lead *disciple*. The key qualification is a desire to be more like Jesus and to see others set free to be fruit-bearing disciples of God! This is not just a course to run for ten weeks. It is a potentially life-changing experience for everyone who attends. As such it is well worth taking time and effort to plan your course rather than rushing into it.

It is designed to be run in the context of a church or Christian community and can work in almost any setting. It works well, for example, in homes, coffee shops, and outreach settings.

It's important to have full support of the main leaders. This can take time to obtain but is worth prayerfully waiting for. The very best practice is for your leaders to go through *disciple* (or the *Freedom In Christ Course* it is based on) and have a freedom appointment first too.

The course will almost run itself. However, we cannot emphasize strongly enough that you need to have gone through the teaching beforehand so that you really understand the material, how it works and really own the truths in it for yourself. It is particularly important that you have gone through *The Steps To Freedom In Christ*, ideally in a personal appointment. This will ensure your own personal freedom, give you the experience of being vulnerable before God, teach you how it works, and give you integrity when you ask others to go through the process. Trust us: it just never works quite as well when those leading haven't been though the Steps first.

And finally, pray. It is striking that the courses that run the best are the ones that are saturated in prayer. Remember discipling people is a spiritual exercise not just an academic one and so prayer is key. We have included some helpful prayers and declarations at the end of this section that will direct your prayers in the weeks before you start the course.

Here are our top tips for preparing to lead *disciple*:

Go through the teaching in the course for yourself

The very best way of preparing yourself to lead *disciple* is to go through it for yourself or to go through *The Freedom In Christ Course* that it is based on. You may be able to sit in on a course at another church or you could simply watch the DVDs.

Have a personal *Steps To Freedom In Christ* appointment

A critical part of your own preparation is to experience *The Steps To Freedom In Christ* for yourself. It sends a powerful message to participants that "this is for everyone" when the leader says, "I did it and I benefitted from it." Ideally, this is something that you will go through in your own church, but, if that is not possible, Freedom In Christ can often put leaders in touch with a local church that will be happy to serve them in this way, provided that it is with a view to running a course in their own church.

Work out and use a "stronghold-buster"

"Stronghold-Busting" is a strategy to renew your mind that is a key element of *disciple*. If you are able to speak from personal experience about how you have used it in your own life, the impact on participants will be that much greater and they will be more likely to use it.

Register with Freedom In Christ

The objective of Freedom In Christ Ministries is to equip Christian leaders to help their people live in freedom and grow in Christ. If you are a leader, we recommend that you register with us as a user of this course. You will receive news, hints and tips, and access to a special section of our website. Registering is free of charge and can be done at www.ficm.org.uk/register.

Have fun!

But most of all have fun! God has amazing things planned for you in the days ahead. We're convinced that *disciple* can make a huge impact as people take hold of the freedom Jesus brings, and start to reach their potential to transform the world in His Name.

Your leadership style

Millennials look for role models who exude humility and authenticity and treat them as equals rather than strong leaders who drive them forward. So rather than seeing yourself as the "expert" telling people what to do and what to believe, it's much better to understand your role as that of a **facilitator** travelling through this together with your participants on a collaborative learning journey.

This is very like the role of a shepherd in New Testament times. These days we drive sheep from behind with dogs and quad bikes. In Jesus' day, the shepherd would stand in front of the flock and call the sheep – they would come and follow of their own free choice. The teachers that millennials follow are servant-hearted, humble, caring, and authentic – basically Christ-like! Please don't think this is an impossible ideal. If you love Jesus and have a heart to see others come closer to Him you're in the right place.

To avoid a top down teaching/preaching model, we haven't included scripts for you to teach yourself but envisage you will use the DVDs.

So we suggest that you go through the course "with" the group. The best way to engage them is to be engaged yourself, debate with them and wrestle with the topics yourself. Millennials need to "own" stuff for themselves, they won't simply believe it because you say it's true, so the discussion times are absolutely key. Don't be tempted to cut them out or cut them short because this is where the learning really happens.

During the discussion times if you can be open and honest about your own journey you will find that openness brings openness, vulnerability brings vulnerability.

The running theme of *disciple* is the participants' life stories. This can be an exciting chapter in their life stories and an exciting chapter in your life story as you facilitate this for them. It doesn't matter how many times you teach this material, God always does something in our own hearts, He may show us an area where we are being deceived or take a key truth a little deeper in to our hearts – whatever it is try to be open and willing for God to do a work in you at the same time as He is doing a work in the lives and hearts of those you are taking through the course!

Leading discussions

The discussion components of *disciple* are a crucial element of the course. This is almost certainly where the key learning will take place.

If your group is larger than six, split people down into sub-groups of no more than five or six for the discussions and mix the groups up each week. The Reflect components should generally be done in twos and threes.

As a leader of a discussion group, one of your main roles is to try to get others to talk. Don't be afraid of silences.

In addition to the questions given, you could start any Chat with the following open questions:

- What do you think about what you have just heard?
- Was there anything you heard that you didn't understand or that needs further clarification?
- How do you think what you have heard applies to you?

Try not to let the conversation wander too far from the main points and keep an eye on the time.

Draw the discussion to a close at the appropriate time by summarizing briefly. The session notes in this Leader's Guide will be helpful here.

Preparing through prayer

Prayer is vital in seeing God's best come out of *disciple*. It expresses your dependence on God alone and brings Him into every aspect of your course. There are two aspects to this:

Personal Prayer

It is important that we keep ourselves in good shape spiritually so that God can work through us each time we lead the course, lead a small group, or teach the material. Let's get into the habit of confessing any sin that could prevent us being in unbroken fellowship with God and taking back any ground we've given to the enemy. In Ephesians 6, we're encouraged to stand firm in the armour of God, and to keep praying for the saints (that is each other), particularly for those attending *disciple*. A suggested prayer you can use is on the next page.

Declarations

It's good to remind ourselves that we are in a spiritual battle when we are helping others become fruitful disciples. But it is a battle in which we hold all the cards. We are children of God seated with Christ in the heavenly realms! However, we need to exercise our authority.

Spiritual effectiveness increases as unity deepens so we encourage you to think "team" as you run the *disciple* and be well prepared together. A suggested declaration for you and others on your team to speak out together is on pages 222–223. When you use it before each session, you will be using YOUR spiritual authority IN CHRIST, and standing TOGETHER on what He's already done, and also on what He's promised to do. From Session 6 onwards, we will also encourage participants to engage in a declaration at the start of each session (see page 90).

PERSONAL PRAYER

God, You're the bedrock under my feet and I depend completely on You. You protect me and clear the ground under me so that my footing is firm. You're the one true and living God. You're a tower of salvation, a shield to all who trust in You, my refuge and my deliverer.

I humbly accept your call to lead this *disciple* course. On my own I can do nothing whatsoever that will make a difference but I stand in the truth that all authority in heaven and earth has been given to the resurrected Christ, and because I'm in Christ, I share that authority in order to make disciples and set prisoners free.

Thank you that you have cleansed me and washed away my sin. As I declare Your Word in Your strength and power, please fill me afresh with Your Holy Spirit.

Strengthen me by Your Spirit, so that I'll be able to take in to a greater degree the extravagant dimensions of Your love and grace and pass that on to others on the course.

I declare that I have a spirit of power and love and a sound mind, and that the Word of Christ dwells in me richly. I've been made holy by Your Word of Truth. The anointing I've received from You abides in me.

Your Word is an indispensable weapon to me, and in the same way, prayer is essential in ongoing warfare. So I declare that because I've made You my dwelling place, no evil shall come upon me. Your promise is that You'll give Your angels charge over all that concerns me, and You'll keep me in all my ways.

I welcome the kingdom of the Lord Jesus Christ afresh today into my life, my home, my family, my work, and into all I do within the ministry of making disciples in my church.

I pray all of this in the name of Jesus Christ. Amen.

(Based on: 1 John 4:4; 2 Samuel 22; Psalm 51; Psalm 19:14; Ephesians 3:16; 2 Timothy 1:7; Colossians 3:16; John 17:17; 1 John 2:27; Ephesians 3:8; Psalm 91:9–11; 2 Corinthians 4:1–7.)

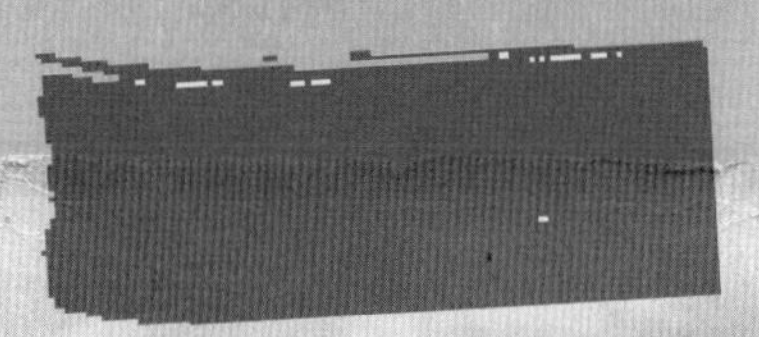

TEAM DECLARATION

We declare that Jesus is our Lord. He's greater than he that's in the world and He came to destroy all the devil's works, having triumphed over them by the cross.

We declare that God has given us *disciple* at this time to share His Word, and the gates of hell will NOT prevail against it. The words that come out of God's mouth will not return empty-handed. They'll do the work He sent them to do.

As those who are seated in the heavenly realms, we agree that Satan and every enemy of the Lord Jesus must not in any way interfere with the running of this *disciple* course. We commit the place where the sessions will take place to Jesus. We cleanse it in Jesus' name from any impure thing.

We declare that the truth of God's mighty Word will be planted and established in [name your church or organization] and our generation will know the truth and be set free.

We'll use our powerful God-tools for tearing down barriers erected against the truth of God, and for building lives of obedience into maturity.

We announce that what God has promised gets stamped with the "yes" of Jesus. We declare that our God can do anything – far more than we could ever imagine or guess or request. Glory to God in the Church! Glory down all the generations forever and ever!

God is striding ahead of us. He's right there with us. He won't let us down. He won't leave us. We won't be intimidated and we won't worry. The battle belongs to Him!

(Based on: Colossians 2:15; John 10:10; John 8:32; Matthew 16:18; Isaiah 55:11; 2 Corinthians 10:4; 2 Corinthians 1:20; Ephesians 3; Deuteronomy 31:8, 1 Samuel 17:47.)

Session notes

01 LEADER'S NOTES

Your unwritten autobiography

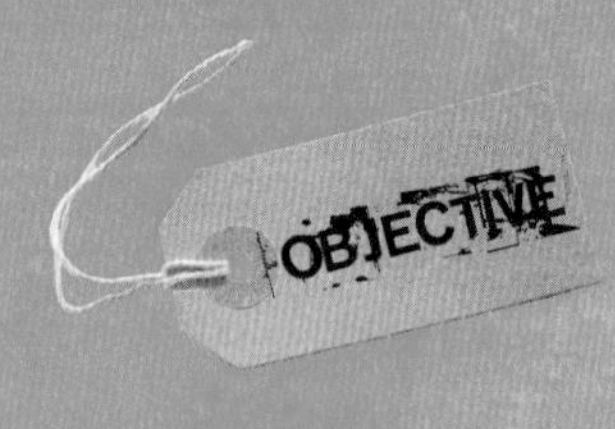

The notes for participants start on page 11.

This session is about showing people that, if they're a Christian, they already have everything they need for their life to make an impact that will last for ever. It then challenges them to consider whether that's what they actually want.

The session is focused around the first part of the parable of the two sons, Luke 15:11–24, which is quoted in full on page 18. The last few verses summarize what we want participants to grasp:

"But the father said to his servants, 'Quick! Bring the best robe and put it on him. Put a ring on his finger and sandals on his feet. Bring the fattened calf and kill it. Let's have a feast and celebrate. For this son of mine was dead and is alive again; he was lost and is found.' So they began to celebrate." (Luke 15:22–24)

The key messages we want participants to take away are:

- God has a superb, outrageously amazing plan for your life.
- You already have everything you need to make it happen if you have become a child of God.
- No one is too messed up to fulfil the plans God has for them.
- It's not about how hard you try but what flows from your relationship with Jesus.
- However, it's by no means inevitable that you'll leave an eternal legacy – and making the choice to do so goes right against the prevailing culture.
- There are things that will hold you back if you let them. But *disciple* will help you work out what they are and how to overcome them – every time.

INTRODUCTION

Introduce yourself (and your team if you have one). Say why you are excited about *disciple*. Are there any testimonies from a previous course that can be shared?

Explain briefly what the session is about (you could have someone read "The Start" on page 10 and "Why?" on page 12 or summarize the opposite page in your own words). Then mention the following:

- This is not a course where you just sit back and listen but a journey that we are going to travel through together.
- There is no pressure to engage in the discussions if you don't want to, but that's often where the real learning takes place so you will be helping everyone else if you do.
- Agree together that anything shared in the group stays in the group and is not discussed elsewhere. This helps people feel at ease and often encourages shyer members to share.
- Recommend that they download the *disciple* app and explain a bit about it (see page 7).

Distractions

If participants constantly feel the need to check their phones, consider introducing the "phone challenge". Everyone has to silence their phones and put them in a pile in the middle of the room. The first person to check their phone before the end of the session has to do a forfeit: perhaps to buy a drink for everyone later or to bake a cake for the next session!

WORSHIP

Lead a short time of worship to ensure that Jesus is at the centre of your meeting.

PRAYER

Dear Heavenly Father,
Thank You for bringing us together to journey through Your word. Thank You that You are already here and receive us with love. We pray that You would pour out Your Holy Spirit and fill us completely. Please show us the amazing plans You have for our lives. Please open our eyes and hearts to the truth of who You are and help us to lay down any preconceived ideas we may have about You.
In Jesus' name. Amen.

STARTER FILM – DVD

The Starter Film raises the question, "What do you want from life?" And this is a great introduction to the course as that is fundamentally the challenge we pose all the way through.

The questions after the film are designed to lead to a discussion that gives people an opportunity to get to know each other. Our suggestion is that you break people into groups of four or five for this.

Remember this part of *disciple* is not about teaching but is primarily to encourage discussion so resist the temptation to leap in and teach.

KEY ONE – DVD

In this session Rob begins to explore the reality that God has plans for your life but you have a choice whether to follow them or not. This can be a real revelation to many, especially to those with a church background who may have come to feel that serving God is a slavish thing we *must* do rather than a choice we have. Too often people will view God with the same lens that they view their earthly father – if their father was stern or demanded obedience they may see God like this and this can hinder their relationship with Him.

Rob then talks about the fact that the millennial generation is the most narcissistic ever because all of our decisions are essentially about us. Obviously this is in direct opposition to the gospel. Many will never have stopped and thought about this before. The result of this attitude is that millennials strive for happiness and things but Rob makes the point that worldly things and achievements will never be enough for us in the end, which sets the scene for an interesting debate.

CHAT TIME ONE – PARTICIPANT'S GUIDE

Here is where the learning happens. The Participant's Guide has some key questions to discuss in groups of two to four people.

This first chat is deliberately light and fun. The main aim is to encourage the group to chat freely and openly because the best learning environment is one where participants gel as a group and get to know each other. There are no right or wrong answers – this is about getting people thinking about their life story so far and where they want it to head from this point.

Before you move on, do encourage participants to write down their answers to the questions on page 16. We will be looking back at them in a later session (though there is no need to mention that).

KEY TWO – DVD

Millennials live in a hedonistic society which says you can watch porn, sleep around, do drugs, and drink yourself into oblivion and it's OK. Jess has a life story that begins similarly to so many millennials who haven't known God. It is a modern true life version of the younger son in Luke 15 which is the focus of this session. She makes clear that no one has messed up too badly to make their life count as a disciple of Jesus from this point forward and that the minute you come to faith, you have everything you need to do that.

The likelihood is that some of the group will have a similar background so don't be surprised how much this story resonates with them. They may really struggle to understand that God isn't mad at them for their past mistakes, especially if they come from a heavily churched background and have rebelled against it. But once they really grasp God's unconditional love, it will transform them.

CHAT TIME TWO – PARTICIPANT'S GUIDE

Encourage participants to reflect in twos and threes on the story they have just heard and how it's changed their view of God. Encourage them to make notes and use the Participant's Guide as their journal as they go through the course. The story is printed on page 18 so they don't need to spend time looking it up if they want to read it again.

KEY THREE – DVD

David looks at the older brother in the story and makes clear that it's not about what you *do*, it's about who you *are* as a child of God. This can really resonate with millennials who have been Christians for a while but have slipped into a theology of works and feeling that they have to earn God's love.

David gives people the opportunity to give their lives to Jesus. Do take a moment to check if anyone would like to do this or indeed has done it during the DVD. It's not uncommon for people to become Christians on Freedom In Christ courses, especially when they are confronted with the grace of God as they are in this session. If they have, then do cover them in prayer over the coming weeks and encourage them to become part of a church.

REFLECT

Have participants spend some time in quiet on their own (you might like to have some instrumental music playing quietly) to consider the questions on page 24 and to write down things they believe may be holding them back.

Take some time to refer them to the "Faulty Thinking Versus What God Says" section on pages 190–191 and encourage them to list there one or two areas from today's session where they realize that what they have believed about God or themselves is not in line with what God actually says in the Bible. It would be helpful to give them an example and emphasize the importance of this exercise.

CONCLUDING REMARKS

Point out the Going Deeper section on page 25 and encourage people to find 20–30 minutes before the next session to go through it.

Remind them to download the app so that they get the daily nuggets of teaching and can watch the Starter Film for the next session beforehand if they want to. Show them how to set up the daily messages by entering the dates of your meetings.

disciple is based on the belief that the Bible is true and is the very word of God Himself. This can be quite a leap for new Christians or non-Christians in the millennial generation who struggle to accept that there is an absolute truth. Recommend that they watch the extra film **"Why Believe The Bible?"** that is accessible via the app, in which Rob shows why it's perfectly reasonable to accept that the Bible is God's message to us. In fact this would be good for everyone as it will give more mature Christians pointers on how to discuss this issue with non-believers.

Be sure not to give the impression that people *have to* do any of the above! It's all entirely optional and if someone doesn't do any of it, that's absolutely fine.

CLOSING PRAYER

Heavenly Father,
Thank You that You love us more than we can ever imagine. Your thoughts about us are as countless as the grains of sand on the beach, and as a shepherd carries a lamb You carry us close to Your hearts. Thank You that You're not distant, angry, or never satisfied with what we do. You know everything about us: when we get up; when we go to bed; and every thought that goes through our minds. And even though You know everything about us, You delight in us, adore us and love us more than we can imagine. Help us, Father, to know this deep in our being and please give us good safe journeys home and a restful night's sleep.
In Jesus' name. Amen.

02 LEADER'S NOTES

How the story starts

The notes for participants start on page 27.

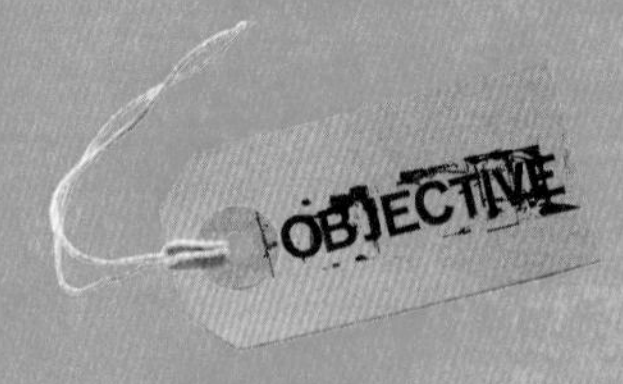

This session starts with the story of Adam and Eve and looks at how their sin left us all being born spiritually dead yet with a driving need to get back to the place of significance, security, and acceptance that God created us for. We then understand the amazing truth that, now that we have become new creations in Christ, that need is met because everything has changed for us. We have a new identity: we are no longer spiritual orphans but are holy ones, beloved children of God! And on that basis, our stories can change too. These are the key Bible verses:

Therefore, if anyone is in Christ, he is a new creation. The old has passed away; behold, the new has come. (2 Corinthians 5:17 ESV)

Whoever has the Son has life; whoever does not have the Son of God does not have life. (1 John 5:12)

The key messages we want participants to take away are:

- When they sinned, Adam and Eve messed things us for us.
- As a result we were born spiritually dead, disconnected from God, and living like spiritual orphans with a burning need to be accepted, significant, and secure.
- When we came to Christ our stories changed forever because Jesus came to give us back the spiritual life that Adam lost.
- We are now part of God's story.
- We are now spiritually alive, holy ones with the ability to do amazing things.
- God loves us no matter what we do.
- We are not saved by how we behave but by what we believe.
- Who we are dictates what we do.

INTRODUCTION

You could invite people to share briefly anything that particularly struck them from the last session or what they are hoping will come from the rest of the course.

This would be a good point to make sure that participants have the date of your *Steps To Freedom In Christ* retreat in their calendars. Tell them that it's a straightforward, matter-of-fact process just between them and God and that we will explain more about it as we go through *disciple*. Refer them to the extra film on the app that introduces the Steps.

In this session we will come across the first of three "Truth Encounter" lists. These are powerful lists of biblical truth that we encourage people to dwell on and read out loud. The first list is called "Who I Am In Jesus" and is on pages 39–41. We have postcards of the lists available that many find really helpful. If you are using the postcards, make sure that you have the Who I Am In Jesus postcard available to distribute at the appropriate time.

WORSHIP

Lead a short time of worship.

PRAYER

Dear Heavenly Father,
Thank You that You are here already. We ask You to fill us with Your Holy Spirit and teach us the truth of who we really are. Help us to share together as we journey through this session and learn these wonderful truths and enable us to take hold of them for ourselves so that we can live out of our real identity.
In Jesus' name. Amen.

STARTER FILM – DVD

This Starter Film raises the question, "who are you?" and looks at how, in the greatest case of identity theft ever, we had our true God-given identity stolen from us.

For the discussion time afterwards, you could keep everyone together for the first question (as long as your group is not too large) and break them into threes or fours for the second question. The discussion is undirected and not designed for teaching. It would be helpful to think in advance about what you would say to the second question.

A Red Herring?

The story of Adam and Eve can be a stumbling block to some people who see it as a fable or illustrative story. For this course it is not critical that people take it as literal fact as long as they accept that God is communicating important truth through it – namely that, through the sin of our first ancestors, we lost the spiritual life and deep sense of significance, security, and acceptance that we were meant to have.

KEY ONE – DVD

Jess looks at the reality that we are spiritual beings not just physical beings. This is a key principle people need to grasp in order to make sense of the rest of the course.

She then looks at Genesis 2 and 3 to unpack how God created man and woman to be born spiritually alive and connected to God with a deep sense of security, significance, and acceptance; and how at the fall the greatest case of identity theft ever happened when we lost our spiritual life and with it the sense of security, significance and acceptance that God intended us to have.

So many of the problems that millennials face are rooted in seeking their security, significance, and acceptance outside of God. The peer pressure they feel to conform to the world and its ways, the striving for success, the pressure to conform to media trends and images, the need to be thin and beautiful all come from trying to meet this legitimate need outside of God.

Jess touches on the way this feeds into the rampant consumerism amongst millennials – the first generation actually to define themselves as consumers. Consumeristic attitudes are in direct opposition to the gospel and need to be challenged.

CHAT TIME ONE – PARTICIPANT'S GUIDE

Here is an opportunity for the group to start to wrestle with this key teaching and look at how our ancestors can affect us today. Encourage people not to spend too long on the first two questions but to focus on the final one.

KEY TWO – DVD

Here Rob unpacks how Jesus restores our spiritual life (John 10:10, John 5:12, John 11:25), which is so much more than simply a "get out of hell free card". It's in this section that we look at who we really are – that, through God's grace, we are now new creations (2 Corinthians 5:17) and holy ones.

This can be a challenge to grasp in a generation where casual sex, abortion, self-harm, eating disorders, binge drinking, drugs, porn, etc. are at an epidemic level. When millennials come to faith they can feel a strong conviction and sense that their past is defining them, that they are still in some way unclean because of their past choices. It's vital that they own the truth that they really are a completely new creation in Christ, that they are holy and pure no matter what they have done or what has been done to them. This is such a critical principle because how they see themselves will determine how they behave.

CHAT TIME TWO – PARTICIPANT'S GUIDE

So the idea that we have been made holy at the deepest level of being can be tough to believe. But if we see ourselves as sinners we are far more likely to sin because that, after all, is what sinners do. Holy ones, on the other hand, are much more likely to live a righteous life.

It's not just people who have been entrenched in the world that find this hard to grasp. It can also be a particularly difficult concept for those with a strong church background where they have adopted a teaching that they are nothing more than a "sinner saved by grace". David goes into this more in the next session but this will be an important chat time for participants.

The third question is profound and worth spending time on. When you discover God's grace, far from thinking that you can now simply go and sin, you want to do everything you can to thank Him and work for Him. And if you don't, then you haven't really understood grace! God has always wanted people who serve Him because they choose to, not because they have to.

Refer people to page 34 where some of the amazing verses are listed about who we now are. If they struggle with this section do encourage them to explore it further in their own time and encourage everyone to add to the list as they come across other verses during the course.

KEY THREE – DVD

In this session David continues to emphasize the fact that we are holy and have no condemnation. This is vital because what we believe about ourselves will always affect the way we behave. If you see yourself as a sinner – you're going to sin. But if you see yourself as a saint who sometimes sins you're far less likely to make the wrong choices.

He also introduces the first of our three "Truth Encounter" lists, "Who I Am In Jesus" (pages 39–41) and invites people to read them out loud together – the words will appear on the screen. Some may feel awkward doing that but do encourage them to join in as it can be a very powerful experience and it's something that churches have done for two thousand years.

The truths in the "Truth Encounter" lists will transform participants' walk with God so do encourage them to spend more time looking at them at home or, better still, to read them out loud every day. The lists are so important that they feature in the app and you can also get them on postcards to hand out to participants.

REFLECT

This is an opportunity for the group to wrestle with this key list, look at what has surprised them and understand where their beliefs haven't been in line with the truth.

Having people get into twos and read the list to each other is an incredibly powerful exercise and we suggest you do this if at all possible.

CONCLUDING REMARKS

Remind people to write areas of faulty thinking that have come to light in the "Faulty Thinking Versus What God Says" section on pages 190–191.

Even though it's the end of this session it's important not to rush this bit and to encourage them to continue it at home over the coming week. Do point out the Going Deeper section in the Participant's Guide too where they are encouraged to do more work with the list and read it out every day.

CLOSING PRAYER

Heavenly Father,
It can be so hard to grasp that we really are holy and pure because of Jesus when we so often don't feel that way. But You are not a man who lies but God who is truth. Help us to see ourselves as we really are and to understand that what we have done doesn't define us. What defines us is what Jesus did, His life, His death and His resurrection. Thank You that we live by grace as Your holy and pure children. Father, please get us home safely and give us a peaceful night's rest as we digest the truth of who we really are.
In Jesus' name. Amen.

I renounce the lie that I am rejected, unloved, dirty, or shameful because in Jesus I am completely ACCEPTED. God says that:

I am God's child [see John 1:12]
I am Jesus' friend [see John 15:15]
I have been justified [see Romans 5:1]
I am united with God and I am one spirit with Him [see 1 Corinthians 6:17]
I have been bought with a price: I belong to God [see 1 Corinthians 6:19–20]
I am a member of Jesus' body [see 1 Corinthians 12:27]
I am a saint, a holy one [see Ephesians 1:1]
I have been adopted as God's child [see Ephesians 1:5]
I have direct access to God through the Holy Spirit [see Ephesians 2:18]
I am forgiven of all my sins [see Colossians 1:14]
I am complete in Jesus [see Colossians 2:10]

I renounce the lie that I am guilty, unprotected, alone, or abandoned because in Jesus I am totally SECURE. God says that:

I am free forever from condemnation [see Romans 8:1–2]
I am assured that all things work together for good [see Romans 8:28]
I am free from all condemning charges against me [see Romans 8:31–34]
I cannot be separated from the love of God [see Romans 8:35–39]
I have been established, anointed, and sealed by God [see 2 Corinthians 1:21–22]
I am confident that the good work God has begun in me will be perfected [see Philippians 1:6]
I am a citizen of heaven [see Philippians 3:20]
I am hidden with Jesus in God [see Colossians 3:3
I have not been given a spirit of fear, but of power, love, and a sound mind [see 2 Timothy 1:7]
I can find grace and mercy to help me when I need [see Hebrews 4:16]
I am born of God and the evil one cannot touch me [see 1 John 5:18]

I renounce the lie that I am worthless, inadequate, helpless, or hopeless because in Jesus I am deeply SIGNIFICANT. God says that:

I am the salt of the earth and the light of the world [see Matthew 5:13–14]
I am a branch of the true vine, Jesus, a channel of His life [see John 15:1–5]
I have been chosen and appointed by God to bear fruit [see John 15:16]
I am a personal, Spirit empowered witness of Jesus [see Acts 1:8]
I am a temple of God [see 1 Corinthians 6:16]
I am a minister of reconciliation for God [see 2 Corinthians 5:17–21]
I am God's fellow worker [see 2 Corinthians 6:1]
I am seated with Jesus in the heavenly realms [see Ephesians 2:6]
I am God's workmanship, created for good works [see Ephesians 2:10]
I can come to God with freedom and confidence [see Ephesians 3:12]
I can do all things through Jesus who strengthens me [see Philippians 4:13]
I am not the great "I Am", but by the grace of God I am what I am [see Exodus 3:14; John 8:24, 28, 58; 1 Corinthians 15:10]

03 LEADER'S NOTES

A true story

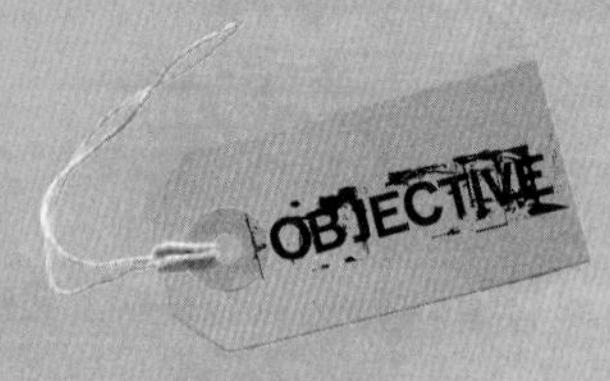

The notes for participants start on page 45.

This session is about the nature of faith. We want participants to understand that faith is choosing to believe in Jesus as the truth rather than simply following feelings. This is vital for millennials who can be prone to follow what they feel and who are therefore sorely tempted to give up on God when life gets hard.

The key verse is John 14:6 (NASB) where Jesus says, "I am the way, and the truth, and the life; no one comes to the Father but through Me."

The main points we want to put across are:

- Our culture makes it hard for us to accept that there is such a thing as absolute truth.
- Yet, if some things are true, then, by definition, other things are not true and there can't be multiple conflicting truths.
- Jesus is <u>the</u> truth.
- Christian faith is simply making a choice to believe what He says is true.
- Faith boils down to finding out from God's Word what is already true and choosing to believe it.
- We will need to keep doing this, even when life is hard, knowing that God has promised that He is working all things together for good (Romans 8:28).
- The effectiveness of faith does not come down to how strong it is but depends on the power and reliability of what you put your faith in.
- Growing in faith is about growing in our relationship with God – we can all grow.

INTRODUCTION

You might like to ask people to share very briefly how they are finding *disciple*. It would be especially helpful to hear from those who have used the *disciple* app.

Remind everyone about the date of your *Steps To Freedom In Christ* retreat and assure them again that it's a straightforward, matter-of-fact process just between them and God. Refer them to the extra film on the app that introduces the Steps.

In this session we come across the second of our three "Truth Encounter" lists. It is called "The Can Do List" and is on 56–57. If you are using the postcards, make sure that you have them available to distribute at the appropriate time.

WORSHIP

Lead a short time of worship.

PRAYER

Dear Heavenly Father,
Thank You that You're here with us already. Please fill us with Your Holy Spirit and help us to understand the notion of truth. We live in a world that wants to deny it even exists and yet we hunger to know what the truth is. We ask that your Holy Spirit would lead us into all truth and help us see past the cultural blindness that can stop us seeing things as they really are. We declare that our minds are our own and we forbid the enemy from influencing us.
In Jesus' name. Amen.

STARTER FILM – DVD

This Starter Film raises the question, "Is truth true for everyone?" This is a tough issue because millennials are saturated in postmodernism which essentially claims that everyone can have their "own" truth and everyone's truth is equally valid as long as they don't try to impose it on anyone else. University lecturers now report that postmodernism is so rampant that students struggle to say that the holocaust was wrong (though they are happy to say it would be wrong for *them*).

What this means in effect, of course, is that, according to postmodernist thought, there is no such thing as absolute truth – a truth that is true for everyone at all times. Any religion or philosophy that makes claims of absolute truth is immediately treated with suspicion.

Postmodernism is a real stumbling block to evangelism in millennials who don't want to be seen as being bigoted or opinionated when they share the truth about Jesus.

Focus particularly on the first question and get ready for an interesting icebreaking chat after this clip!

KEY ONE – DVD

Rob kicks off this challenging session by discussing the fact that absolute truth is not socially acceptable but then discusses a key question to illustrate the fallacy of postmodernist thinking: "What happens when we die?"

He challenges the notion that something becomes true just because you believe in it. This is a tough one for millennials because society widely accepts that, as long as you don't harm anyone else, it's perfectly OK to choose to believe whatever you want. That is, of course, your choice but what you choose to believe will have consequences for you.

Finally Rob makes the challenging point that Jesus is THE truth.

CHAT TIME ONE – PARTICIPANT'S GUIDE

In this Chat we challenge the postmodern worldview by looking at the concept of absolute truth and discussing John 14:6 (NASB) where Jesus says, "I am the way, and the truth, and the life; no one comes to the Father but through Me." This verse can be a huge challenge to those saturated in postmodernism who would far rather it said, "I am a way, and a truth, and a life." But there is no escaping what Jesus actually said.

In discussing absolute truth , Rob used the illustration of what happens after death and it can be helpful to keep drawing the group back to that. What you believe before you die about what will happen to you after death carries no weight when the moment actually arrives. Logic suggests that we will all experience the same thing no matter what we believed beforehand.

If people are struggling or the conversation gets stuck, it may be worth pausing and inviting the Holy Spirt to come and lead the group into truth.

This is guaranteed to be a fascinating chat time as people in the group wrestle with the concept of truth – have fun!

KEY TWO – DVD

In this section David explores what faith is and how we can grow in it. Some people have the impression that having faith is somehow deciding against the odds to believe something that really isn't true. In fact it's the opposite to that. David makes clear that faith is simply a choice to believe what is in fact already true.

Faith works not because of how much of it we have but because of who we put our faith in: a God who is all powerful (see Matthew 17:20).

Finally David discusses how to grow in faith by spending time with God and in His word and then putting into action what you have learnt (James 2:17–18).

The section includes a testimony from someone who realized that having faith wasn't a question of asking God to do something but was about making a choice.

CHAT TIME TWO – PARTICIPANT'S GUIDE

This Chat starts off with a discussion about the fact that faith is a choice you make. You could perhaps start by asking people whether or not they can identify with the lady who told the story of her struggles with intellectualism until she finally made a choice to believe what God says.

It then moves to encouraging the group to consider how to get to know God better, which is what will increase their faith, and how practically, they could spend more time with God. A key aim of *disciple* is to help participants develop good spiritual habits such as journaling, spending time reading their Bibles, and hanging out with God. We want them to learn to do these things not because they feel they have to out of some sense of religious duty but because they really want to get to know this amazing Father God so much better.

KEY THREE – DVD

In this session Jess shares a raw and honest story about walking by faith when life gets tough. Walking with God is not a guarantee that everything will feel nice and be easy but it is a guarantee that God will help you through what life throws at you and will use the trials of life to bring personal growth and fruit (Romans 8:2) which will help you fulfil the goal of becoming more and more like Jesus in character.

This is a key session as millennials tend to make decisions based on how they feel and give up really quickly when life gets tough. They often believe that the goal of their faith is to make life easy and happy so when things go into reverse they deduce that faith in God doesn't work. For them to grow as disciples this needs to be recognized in their own lives and challenged.

The reality is that, if a member of the group hasn't yet gone through major life difficulties, they will at some point. Jess offers a prayer for people to commit to depending on God no matter what life throws at them. We would suggest you invite everyone to engage with this prayer during the DVD session.

Finally Jess introduces the second "Truth Encounter" list which is called "The Can Do List". It is on pages 56–57 in the Participant's Guide and will also come up on the screen. Encourage people to read it out loud together when it appears.

Encourage people to spend more time at home with the "Truth Encounter" lists, ideally reading them out loud every day. Remember, the lists are so important that they also feature in the app and you can get them on postcards to hand out to participants.

1. Why should I say I can't do it when the Bible says I can do all things through Jesus who gives me strength (Philippians 4:13)?
2. Why should I lack when I know that God will supply all my needs according to His riches in glory in Jesus (Philippians 4:19)?
3. Why should I be afraid when the Bible says God has not given me a spirit of fear, but one of power, love, and a sound mind (2 Timothy 1:7)?
4. Why should I lack faith to complete my calling knowing that God has given me a measure of faith (Romans 12:3)?
5. Why should I be weak when the Bible says that God is the strength of my life and that I will be strong and take action because I know Him (Psalm 27:1; Daniel 11:32)?
6. Why should I allow Satan supremacy in my life when He that is in me is greater than he that is in the world (1 John 4:4)?
7. Why should I accept defeat when the Bible says that God always leads me in victory (2 Corinthians 2:14)?
8. Why should I be without wisdom when Christ became wisdom to me from God and God gives me wisdom generously when I ask Him for it (1 Corinthians 1:30; James 1:5)?
9. Why should I be depressed when I can remember God's loving kindness, compassion and faithfulness and have hope (Lamentations 3:21–23)?
10. Why should I worry when I can cast all my anxiety on Jesus who cares for me (1 Peter 5:7)?
11. Why should I ever be in bondage when I know that, where the Spirit of God is, there is freedon (2 Corinthians 3:17; Galatians 5:1)?
12. Why should I feel guilty when the Bible says I an guilty because I am in Jesus (Romans 8:1)?
13. Why should I feel alone when Jesus said He is wi me always and He will never leave me or let me g (Matthew 28:20; Hebrews 13:5)?
14. Why should I feel cursed or that I am the victim of bad luck when the Bible says that Jesus redeemed me from the curse of the law that I can receive His Spirit (Galatians 3:13–14)?
15. Why should I be discontent when, like Paul, I can learn to be content in all my circumstances (Philippians 4:11)?
16. Why should I feel worthless when Jesus became sin for me so that I could become the righteousness of God in Him (2 Corinthians 5:21)?
17. Why should I have a persecution complex knowing that nobody can be against me when God is for me (Romans 8:31)?
18. Why should I be confused when God is the author of peace and gives me knowledge through the Holy Spirit who lives in me (1 Corinthians 14:33; 1 Corinthians 2:12)?
19. Why should I feel like a failure when I am a conqueror in all things through Jesus (Romans 8:37)?
20. Why should I let the pressures of life bother me when I can take courage knowing that Jesus has overcome the world and its tribulations (John 16:33)?

REFLECT

These final thoughts focus on "The Can Do List" and encourages the group to highlight the truths that most surprised them or that stood out the most. Highlighting them can be helpful so that they can return to them again later.

Point them to the Going Deeper section on page 59 which encourages them to work more with the list.

Take a moment of quiet to allow the Holy Spirit to highlight to participants areas of their belief system that are not in line with truth and remind them to record them on pages 190–191.

CONCLUDING REMARKS

Jess has talked openly about debt and bankruptcy in this session. This is a huge issue with millennials who believe that they need to keep up their image by having all the latest trends in technology, cars, etc. As a result, many are drowning in debt but don't talk about it. If this session causes people to open up about money issues, it would be good to encourage them that this is a good time for them to deal with it. You could connect them with one of the excellent non-profit organizations that help people take control of their finances.

The Going Deeper section encourages participants to share their struggles in this area with a pastor or Christian friend – one of the joys of the body of Christ is that we don't have to walk alone.

CLOSING PRAYER

Heavenly Father,
Thank You that You are the truth and we simply need to make a choice to believe that. As we go from here, please help us to get to know You better and better. Please open Your Word to us in new and exciting ways – speak to us as we read it and show us more of the truth that it holds. Father, please get us home safely and give us a restful night's sleep.
In Jesus' name. Amen.

04 LEADER'S NOTES

The story of the world

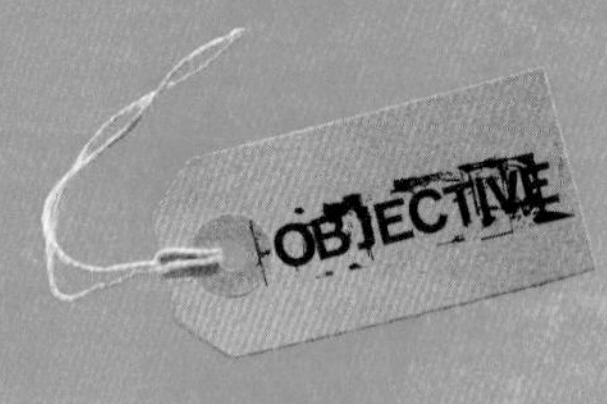

The notes for participants start on page 61.

In the first three sessions we have looked at some basic truths. We now turn our attention to the three enemies that seek to deflect us from these truths: the world, the flesh, and the devil. In this session we will consider the world.

Our main objective is to understand how the world seeks to knock us off track and redirect our path through false promises, the pull of consumerism and comfort, and our worldview which distorts how we see reality.

The key messages we want to communicate are:

- Though our identities are set in Christ, the world battles to influence us to take on false identities and to settle for less from our lives than God wants for us.
- Satan is the ruler of this world.
- The world promises to meet our deep God-given needs for significance, acceptance, and security but ultimately delivers only bondage.
- Issues of comfort and consumerism – what the Bible calls "the lust of the flesh, the lust of the eyes, and the pride of life" – exercise a huge subliminal attraction.
- The truth behind so-called "sexual freedom" and casual sex.
- We need to choose to throw off the worldview we grew up with and take hold of the Biblical worldview which is how things really are.
- Intimate acquaintance with the truth helps us overcome the story of the world.

INTRODUCTION

You might like to ask how people are getting on with the "Truth Encounter" lists. Have people found it helpful to look at them every day? Are they starting to take hold of some of these great truths in their hearts, not just their heads?

Check that people have the date of *The Steps To Freedom In Christ* retreat in their calendars.

WORSHIP

Lead a short time of worship.

PRAYER

Dear Heavenly Father,
Thank You that You're here already and ready to teach us more of Your truth. Please saturate us with Your peace as we look at the world and how it seeks to distract us. The world is so busy and noisy and yet we need to find a quiet place to meet with You and see You for who You really are. Lord, would You make this room a quiet place and speak into our hearts. Please fill us with Your Holy Spirit and help us understand.
In Jesus' name. Amen.

STARTER FILM – DVD

This Starter Film raises the question, "What is real freedom?" It powerfully makes the point that, whilst the world says freedom is the ability to choose, if a choice ends up with you being ensnared in stuff and unable to break free, it isn't freedom at all.

Dan shares his own story of breaking free from an addiction to porn. The probability is that some people in the room will be addicted to porn. It's not likely that they will discuss it in a group situation (and not helpful either) but if anyone does tell you quietly, thank them for their honesty, assure them that it makes no difference to God's love for them, and encourage them that *disciple* will give them everything they need to get free if they really want to.

KEY ONE – DVD

David begins this by introducing us to the world and discusses how it makes false promises to meet our needs for security, significance, and acceptance. The world promises us that if we perform well and accomplish a lot we will be significant; that if we gain status and wealth we will be secure; and that if we look right, fit in, and make others admire us, we will be accepted. But these promises are bankrupt and ultimately fail to deliver and the only way to feel truly significant, secure, and accepted is through spiritual life in Christ.

CHAT TIME ONE – PARTICIPANT'S GUIDE

This Chat is about helping participants recognize the world's false promises in their own lives.

The millennial generation has generally bought heavily into the world's false promises in its quest for comfort, nice feelings, and "things" so participants should find it easy to recognize the world at work in their own lives, even if they choose to discuss examples from other people!

KEY TWO – DVD

Jess focuses on 1 John 2:15–17 which looks at "the lust of the flesh, the lust of the eyes, and the pride of life". She explains that the lust of the flesh is our old programming from before Jesus came. It's the pull to form unhelpful behaviour patterns like comfort eating, retail therapy, and sex outside of marriage.

The lust of the eyes is the pull to look at things that are unhealthy for us like porn or horror.

The pride of life is the pull on us to achieve and then boast about our achievements and possessions.

This is another important session for this generation who can unknowingly be very driven by the world without questioning. They may find it very illuminating if they haven't already recognized these things as a problem in life. And they may well not have done because society doesn't generally see much of a problem with retail therapy, sex outside of marriage, or watching horror and porn. This section touches on some hot topics which the group may want to explore further in the Chat that follows.

CHAT TIME TWO – PARTICIPANT'S GUIDE

The first question deals with sex as God intended. There is some additional teaching on this in an extra film on the *disciple* app (more details below) and we recommend that you watch this before this session. Recommend it to participants too.

We have touched on some sensitive issues such as porn, casual sex, and comfort eating but we have also had the promise that all children of God can overcome this stuff and its effects. So this is likely to be a lively Chat time!

Remind people that, if they are struggling with these things, they really can get free and this course will give them the tools to do that if they stick with it, go through *The Steps to Freedom in Christ*, and then renew their minds.

Not all millennials will see the dangers in retail therapy, what they watch on TV, or casual sex so be prepared for an interesting debate as they wrestle with the notion that these things might be doing them harm.

KEY THREE – DVD

In this section Rob challenges them to recognize that we all have a worldview which distorts our view of reality. He looks at the rise of secular humanism which is the subliminal belief that we are working towards and creating a world that is manmade – essentially we become our own gods.

Secular humanism is rife amongst the millennial generation but many of them will never have recognized it in their culture let alone in their own lives. It's an important revelation for them because it sucks their dependence away from God and breeds pride and striving.

Rob also discusses how, if you're under forty and born in the West, you are likely to have a worldview that is heavily influenced by postmodernism which rejects the notion of absolute truth. Postmodernism, as we have noted, is a real stumbling block to this generation who feel reluctant to share their faith for fear of offending their friends. It's not uncommon to hear young adults saying something like "Jesus is my truth", and this needs to be addressed if they are to go out and make an impact for God with their lives.

Finally Rob looks at how, instead of replacing our old beliefs with the truth in God's Word, we can end up bolting Jesus onto the beliefs that we already hold which leads to a "salad bar" spirituality. This is a symptom of postmodernism and is widespread amongst young adults who are inclined to accept biblical teaching that feels nice but reject the parts of the Bible that challenge them. It also shows itself in a willingness to engage in practices from other religions such as Buddhist meditations.

REFLECT

This Reflect session is best done in twos and threes.

The problem with a worldview is it can be really hard to recognize that you have one until you sit down and compare it to the biblical worldview. If participants are struggling with the concepts, you could get them to think about travel they may have done outside their own culture and how the worldview in other cultures differs from that at home. Once they recognize that they may find it easier to see their own worldview.

Remember to pause and ask them to reflect on any areas of their belief system that have come to light that do not line up with what God says is true and remind them to record these on pages 191–192.

CONCLUDING REMARKS

Point out the Going Deeper section which is essentially a continuation of the thinking they have been doing in the Reflect section. Emphasize the importance of not just recognizing where we have a non-biblical worldview but also taking some action to renounce it and replace it with truth.

Recommend that they watch the extra film presented by Jess and André called **"The Gift Of Sex"** that can be accessed via the app. Sex is such a hot topic for millennials yet so often not touched upon very much in churches that we wanted to devote more time to it.

Millennials have been told not to have sex before marriage but often without being told why. With no reason for the "no", many Christians end up in uncommitted sexual relationships feeling guilty or angry with the Church and its stance. Those without a strong Christian background may have no idea that having multiple sexual partners is harmful to them.

In this extra session Jess and André unpack how sex forms a spiritual bond and how having sex outside a committed marriage relationship causes harm. This isn't a "you mustn't do this or you mustn't do that" approach but outlines powerfully how sex is a beautiful gift from God when it's used in its proper context.

PRAYER

Heavenly Father,
You tell us that we are to be in the world but not of the world. You have made us to be light and salt in the places where we live and work. But it's not easy. Please help us to see how the world contaminates our view of reality and let us see it through Your eyes. We choose to throw out our old worldview and commit ourselves to see things as they really are, as Your Word tells us they are. We want to be growing, fruitful disciples whose lives make a real difference. We give You our bodies as living sacrifices and choose to follow You.
In Jesus' name. Amen.

05 LEADER'S NOTES

The story of the flesh

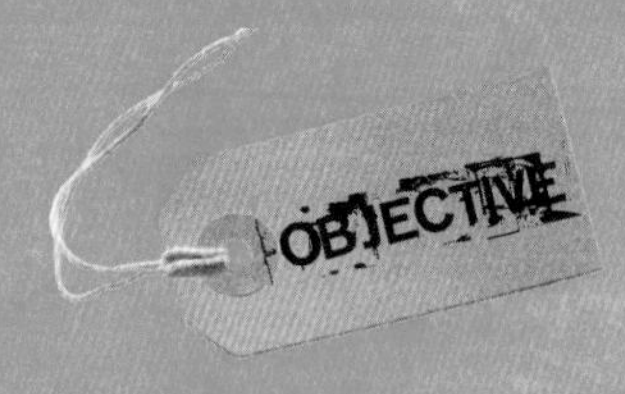

The notes for participants start on page 75.

In this session we look at the second of our enemies that try to pull us away from truth: the flesh. "Flesh" sounds like an old-fashioned term but it's a literal translation of the Greek word "sarx" used in the New Testament which simply means "meat" or "flesh". Some Bible translations have experimented with interpreting it as something like "sinful nature" or "old nature". However, that could easily lead Christians to believe that they still have a nature that is fundamentally sinful whereas, as we have seen in previous sessions, they have become the righteousness of God, are holy ones, and share God's divine nature.

In this session we will liken the flesh to our "default programming". It did not vanish when we became Christians but we have everything we need to overcome it. Instead of listening to the flesh, we can make a choice to walk according to the Holy Spirit which is in direct opposition to it. The key truths we want participants to grasp are:

- Christianity is not a quick-fix. Becoming like Jesus is a process that takes time and requires us to do our part.
- Christian faith is not about getting what we want and just because we may not get what we hope for, it doesn't mean it isn't true.
- When we became Christians our very nature changed and we are now spiritual beings, but the pull of the flesh didn't disappear.
- The Spirit and the flesh are in direct opposition to each other. We can choose either to walk by the Spirit or by the flesh.
- Overcoming the flesh comes down to our own choices.
- As we consistently choose to walk by the Spirit, the fruit of the Spirit will automatically grow in us.
- Self-control is part of the fruit of the Spirit.

INTRODUCTION

You might ask whether anyone has been particularly struck by the truth that, because we are in Jesus, we have become holy ones and ask them to say what it means to them.

WORSHIP

Lead a short time of worship.

PRAYER

Dear Heavenly Father,
We thank You that You are always ready and willing to show us the truth. We're here because we want to grow and become more like You in our character, thoughts, and actions. Please show us the lies we have come to believe and how we can walk by the Spirit and overcome our flesh so that we resemble You more and more each day.
In Jesus' name. Amen.

STARTER FILM – DVD

This Starter Film raises the question, "Are you believing lies?" It begins to open up the issue of things happening to us or being said to us in the past, which might have caused us to believe things that are not true and can hold us back in later life.

Lots of people have been bullied or had terrible things done to them or spoken over them. If this Starter Film brings this up in the undirected chat time it would be good to encourage participants that *disciple* will give them the tools that they need to overcome all that and take hold of their freedom in Christ.

The Steps To Freedom In Christ retreat will be a key day that will help everyone recognize lies they have believed, deal with them, and move on in life. It is a repentance-based process that will help even those who have suffered significant trauma. We would suggest that those people will benefit from going through the Steps one-to-one rather than in a group.

KEY ONE – DVD

Rob discusses how the flesh is what comes naturally to a fallen human. If you repeat a negative behaviour for long enough it will become a habit or stronghold which you will struggle to get free from. It becomes a kind of "programming" or "default behaviour".

It's important to note and to emphasize to participants that the flesh is not part of our core identity. It's not who we are. Rather it is a hangover from our life without God and is in direct opposition to the Spirit (Romans 8:5–7).

A key part of this session is challenging the faulty belief that the goal of faith is to feel good and have a nice life. This is a real issue for millennials who can tend to give up on God too easily when life gets tough. They also tend to expect Christian faith to act like a quick fix where one prayer mends everything. It's vital that they realize that the flesh isn't something that God will just switch off but is something that they overcome in Christ.

CHAT TIME ONE – PARTICIPANT'S GUIDE

This Chat is designed to help people get to grips with what the flesh looks like in their own life.

It then focuses on the lie that the goal of our faith is for everything to feel good and get us everything we want. As this is a key issue or millennials it's sure to be an interesting time. Many of them will never have realized that they have fallen for this lie and yet, when they reflect on it, they may well recognize it in their own lives.

KEY TWO – DVD

Jess looks at 1 Corinthians 2:14 – 3:3 (see page 81) where Paul categorizes people into three types: natural, spiritual, and fleshly. The natural person is someone who is not yet a Christian. The spiritual person is a picture of how we can live now that we are Christians. The fleshly person is a Christian who, instead of listening and following the promptings of the Holy Spirit, is following and listening to the urges of the flesh. Jess then challenges people to work out which type of person they are.

She unpacks what stops people walking by the Spirit: not knowing the truth of who you are and who God really is; being deceived; and unresolved personal and spiritual issues. The aim is that everyone in the group should see that becoming a spiritual person is not some unreachable goal but is completely and utterly achievable.

This is likely to be quite revelatory to a generation that can all too quickly conclude that faith "doesn't work" because a prayer for them to grow or overcome something doesn't seem to have been answered. Jess shows that Jesus has in fact answered that prayer – two thousand years ago! There are things that they need to do and truth that they need to take hold of.

CHAT TIME TWO – PARTICIPANT'S GUIDE

This Chat gives your group the opportunity to respond to the challenge Jess set as to which type of person they think they are. Some people may not be happy to share this with a group and that's absolutely fine. The important thing is that they recognize it for themselves, not that they share it with others.

KEY THREE – DVD

In this session David looks at Matthew 11:18–29 and helps people understand that overcoming the flesh and walking by the Spirit is not about "trying harder" or following a list of religious rules. It's rooted in our relationship with Jesus. This is so important and so refreshing for people when they really "get" it. Many millennials have given up on church because they have perceived it as a religious list of what to do and what not to do. The idea that it's all about a relationship can be very liberating and bring down these stumbling blocks.

David further challenges the faulty belief that faith is about feeling good by clarifying that walking by the Spirit is about living by what is true not what feels good. It's simply a choice, and when we walk by the Spirit, the fruit of the Spirit – including self-control – will become more and more evident in our lives (Galatians 5:22–23).

REFLECT

This Reflect is best done in twos or threes. Remind people to note down on pages 190–191 any lies they realize they have been believing.

CONCLUDING REMARKS

You may like to emphasize that walking by the Spirit is not about trying harder or getting a super anointed person to pray for you. The key thing here is that they connect to the fact that it's all about a relationship with Jesus. Direct them to the Going Deeper section on page 87.

PRAYER

Heavenly Father,
Thank You that none of us needs to continue to walk in the flesh because you have already given us everything we need to walk by the Spirit. We already have every blessing in Jesus. Help us to keep recognizing and overcoming the lies that we have come to believe that are holding us back. Please bless our journey home and give us a peaceful night's rest.
In Jesus' name. Amen.

06 LEADER'S NOTES

The story of the devil

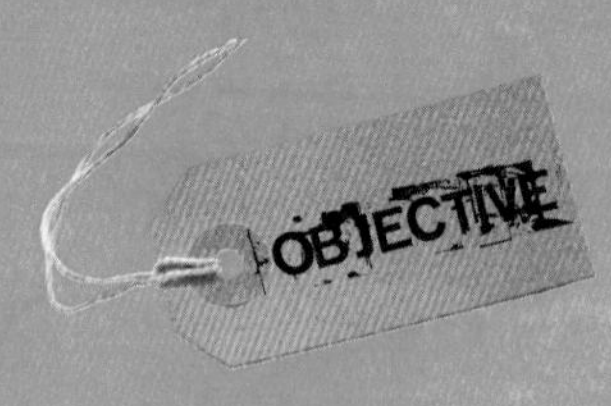

The notes for participants start on page 89.

In this session we focus on our third enemy, the devil. Of the three, the devil is the easiest to deal with but is the one that will probably do you the most harm if you don't.

Put on the full armour of God, so that you can take your stand against the devil's schemes. (Ephesians 6:11)

And having disarmed the powers and authorities, he made a public spectacle of them, triumphing over them by the cross. (Colossians 2:15)

"My prayer is not that you take them out of the world but that you protect them from the evil one. They are not of the world, even as I am not of it. Sanctify them by the truth; your word is truth." (John 17:15–17)

We want participants to understand that the devil is real but is defeated and that we already have everything we need to overcome his lies and make our lives count for something eternal. By becoming aware of his schemes we can ensure we don't fall for his lies. Here are the key points:

- Although Satan has become the ruler of this world, he is just a created being and is not remotely comparable to God, the Creator.
- In Christ we have power and authority to resist him as long as we are submitting to God.
- The devil has only three weapons: temptation, accusation, and deception.
- The battle is for truth and the battleground is our minds.
- The devil can gain influence in our lives through unresolved sin but it's straightforward to take back any ground we have given him.
- We need to be careful we don't inadvertently give him ground through – for example, participating in non-Christian spiritualities that claim to be beneficial.

INTRODUCTION

You will see that the notes in the Participant's Guide for this session are even more packed with Bible verses than usual. Why? Because our Western worldview predisposes us to overlook the reality of the spiritual world. When we read such things in our Bibles, we tend to skip over them, not intentionally but because our worldview means we don't have a "box" to put them in. However, the whole backdrop of the Bible is the battle that is going on between good and evil and it is essential that we develop a good understanding of how it works. If we don't, our tendency will be either to disregard it, with the result that it becomes easy for the enemy to hold us back, or to go overboard in the other direction and ascribe Satan far more power than he actually has, with the result that we become frightened of him. Before you lead this session, we recommend that you take some time to read through the Bible verses and make a conscious effort to bring your belief system into line with them.

You might like to start the session by asking people to share about how they are finding the daily nuggets that come from the *disciple* app.

Remind people about the *Steps To Freedom In Christ* retreat that is coming up between Sessions 8 and 9.

WORSHIP

Lead a short time of worship.

PRAYER

Dear Heavenly Father,
Thank You that all authority and power in heaven and on earth belong to You. Thank You that, because we are Your children, we share in that power and authority. As we start this session, we want to take a moment to give You anything that is on our minds, anything that we are worried about or need to say sorry for. [Pause]. Thank You, Father, that You are completely trustworthy and in control of everything.
In Jesus' name. Amen.

DECLARATION

From this session onwards, we want to encourage participants to make a declaration at the start of each session as well as a prayer. A declaration is different to a prayer in that a prayer is spoken to God whilst a declaration is spoken out loud into the heavenly realms in general. It is a way of exercising the power and authority that we have in Christ. We want participants to know that in Christ they are seated at the right hand of the Father, far above all power and authority and can act accordingly.

Explain the above to the group and then ask them to read out loud together the declaration on page 90. Encourage them to read it loudly and confidently as the children of God they are.

In Jesus' name we declare that God is sovereign. We submit ourselves to God and tell every enemy of the Lord Jesus Christ to leave this place now. We declare that they cannot stop the will of God being done in this group or in our lives. We belong to Jesus and the evil one cannot touch us.

STARTER FILM – DVD

This Starter Film raises the question, "What's holding you back?" and introduces the concept that sin gives the devil footholds and footholds give the devil a right to hold us back. This is likely to be a new concept to some and one that can be difficult to grasp for people who have been influenced by a Western worldview which predisposes us to overlook the reality of the spiritual world in our daily lives even if we acknowledge its existence theologically and intellectually.

In the discussion we want people to start to realize that, if they have been frustrated by their lack of spiritual growth, it might be good to consider the possibility that the enemy may be holding them back because of unresolved sin issues from the past or present.

In the second question the quotation from C. S. Lewis helpfully brings out the two reactions people tend to have to the devil. Either they overlook the reality of the spiritual world because they have been conditioned by the Western worldview. Or else they take too much interest in it and become fearful. This can be down to the influence of non-Western worldviews such as animism or because of the fact that Hollywood and the media love to glamorize evil.

For this reason, try to steer the group away from discussions that risk sensationalizing evil, such as sharing scary stories.

KEY ONE – DVD

In this section, David shows us how Satan is the ruler of this world (John 12:31) and the ruler of the kingdom of the air (Ephesians 2:2) and how the unsaved world lives under his power (1 John 5:19). Satan is called "the father of lies" (John 8:44) and the battle we face is one between truth and lies with the battleground being our minds.

He then goes on to dispel the most common lies that are held about him: that he's not real; that he's equal in power to God; that he's more powerful than we are; and that as Christians we are somehow immune to his schemes.

CHAT TIME ONE – PARTICIPANT'S GUIDE

This Chat continues the theme of the Starter Film discussion and moves on to consider the lies that David has talked about.

The final question is designed to help people start to consider their responsibility in the spiritual battle. People might think that putting on the armour of God is little more than saying a prayer every morning going through each piece of the armour, whereas it's much more about committing to believe and act on the truth, making sure we really know that we have become righteous. You might like to draw participants' attention to the underlinings on page 96 which usefully show that we have a responsibility to "stand". You could ask what that might look like in practice. Note too that when we choose to act in faith – in other words when we act in accordance with God's Word – we can expect to see "all" the enemy's arrows extinguished, not "nearly all"!

Note: we are not saying that every problem we may encounter has a spiritual root. We are whole people – body, soul and spirit – and we need to take the whole of reality into account. We don't want to go looking for a demon behind every bush but neither do we want to overlook the possibility that a demon may be involved. We need to adopt a Biblical worldview.

KEY TWO – DVD

Jess now focuses on how Satan works. She affirms that the battleground is our minds and explains that he only has three strategies to use against us: to tempt, to accuse, and to deceive.

She explains how sin gives the devil a foothold or a place of influence in our lives that can keep us stuck, as we saw in the Starter Film. We can try as hard as we like but, if we have unresolved sin issues, it's hard to move forward in our walk with God.

The good news is that James 4:7 makes clear that if we submit to God and resist the devil we can take back the ground from the enemy and he has to flee from us.

This can be a light bulb moment for members of the group who have been wanting to continue in their Christian journey but feel frustrated and held back. Often they have submitted to God but not resisted the devil. Sometimes they have tried resisting the devil but have not submitted to God. We need to do both or we will remain in bondage. There can be a real breakthrough as they realize that they are not useless or some kind of second-class Christian but can take hold of their freedom and travel onwards.

Finally Jess makes it clear that dabbling in non-Christian spiritualities and faiths can give a foothold to the devil. This is further unpacked in the additional teaching session available via the app – **"The Truth Behind The Occult".** It's likely that some members of the group will have dabbled in the occult in the past. It would be worth reassuring them that they can deal with it all when they go through *The Steps To Freedom In Christ.*

CHAT TIME TWO – PARTICIPANT'S GUIDE

This Chat session encourages participants to recognize that some of the thoughts that come into their mind may not actually be their own. This will be an important revelation for some who act on any thought that appears. It's important to realize that you don't have to simply act on a thought but can step back, evaluate it, and make a choice.

KEY THREE – DVD

In this section Rob considers our defence against the devil's lies. He returns to the subject of the armour of God which featured in the first Chat and the key component that holds everything else together – the belt of truth.

Jesus has promised to build the Church and assured us that Hell cannot stand against it (Matthew 16:18). Christians who submit to God and resist the enemy have absolutely nothing to fear from him!

Finally, Rob makes it clear that our response to all this should not be to focus on the darkness but simply to turn on the light. We are to carry God's light and use truth to counter the devil's lies.

REFLECT

This Reflect is a little different. Ask the group to split into pairs and talk about the short question on deception. Hopefully they will conclude that they probably are being deceived but don't know how. Deception is hard to spot unless the Spirit of Truth guides you and that is exactly how *The Steps To Freedom In Christ* works. Encourage them to spend some time praying together as they prepare for the Steps.

Remind them to record faulty beliefs on pages 190–191. Hopefully they are getting the hang of this now and this session will have underlined the importance of rooting out deception and faulty thinking.

CONCLUDING REMARKS

Point out the Going Deeper section which deals with the other two strategies of the enemy: temptation and accusation.

Recommend that they watch the extra film presented by Jess called **"The Truth Behind The Occult"** that can be accessed via the app. Occult practices are on the rise amongst millennials because they have lost the knowledge that it is dangerous to dabble. They also have a huge hunger for spirituality which means that many are turning to the occult to experience the spiritual without realizing that it will entangle and harm them.

Many have experienced the occult unknowingly because it now appears in things like business training, dressed up as something wholesome or even scientific.

Jess looks at why God forbids occult practices, how you can unknowingly wander into the occult, and how to get free from any occult that you may have knowingly or unknowingly been involved in. This extra session will also equip participants to help others who have become entangled in occult practices.

PRAYER

Heavenly Father,
Thank You that You are light and in You is no darkness at all. Thank You that as Christians we are filled with Your Holy Spirt and Your light. Help us to carry that light out into the world. Thank You that You have seated us in Christ at Your right hand in the heavenly realms – the seat of all power and authority – and that You share that power and authority with us, simply because we are Your children. As we go from here we pray that You will give us all a safe journey home and a peaceful night's sleep.
In Jesus' name. Amen.

07 LEADER'S NOTES

Truth and emotions

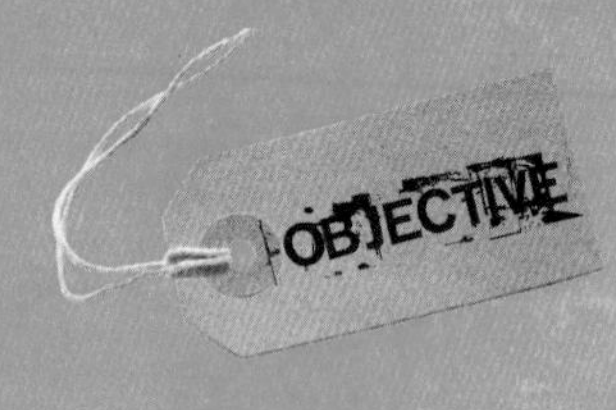

The notes for participants start on page 105.

Emotions are a big deal for this generation. In this session we want participants to understand that God gave us our emotions and that they function as barometers of our spiritual health to enable us to stay on track.

The main points we want them to take away are:

- Emotions are given to us by God for our own good.
- Emotions act as signposts to show what is happening inside.
- We cannot control our emotions but we can change them over time by choosing to change what we can control: our beliefs.
- As we consistently choose to believe what God says, we'll find our emotions will fall into line with the truth.
- If what we believe doesn't reflect truth, our feelings won't reflect reality.
- Being real and honest with God is the only effective way to manage our emotions.
- Life's events don't determine how you feel but your perception of them does.
- We are not a product of our past but of Christ's past: His death on the cross; His resurrection; and His ascension to the right hand of the Father.
- We don't feel our way into good behaviour. We behave our way into good feelings.

INTRODUCTION

The Steps To Freedom In Christ retreat comes up after the next session so this might be a good time to remind people that this is a crucial part of *disciple* and not to be missed.

If someone is unable to attend the retreat, we strongly recommend that you make other arrangements for them to go through *The Steps To Freedom In Christ*. The most obvious way forward for such people would be for you to make arrangements to take them through the process individually. This should be done with a facilitator and a prayer partner of the same gender as the freedom seeker and typically takes three to five hours.

Note: this session raises painful issues for some and specifically touches on the sensitive issue of sexual assault. Sadly sexual assault is all too common and you may have someone in your group that discloses this has happened to them. Please consider in advance how you can offer support to anyone who may need it. Make sure you understand your church's safeguarding and pastoral care policies and act accordingly.

WORSHIP

Lead a short time of worship.

PRAYER

Dear Heavenly Father,
Thank You that You are intimately acquainted with all of our ways, You know what's in our hearts and when others misunderstand, You understand us completely. You see it all and You love us unconditionally. Please help us to understand our emotions and how they can lead us in the wrong direction. Thank You that You're already here, and ready to show us the truth.
In Jesus' name. Amen.

DECLARATION

Remind the group how we learned last time about our power and authority in Christ and ask them to read out loud together the declaration on page 106. Remind them to declare it confidently and boldly as the children of God that they are!

In Jesus' name we declare that God is sovereign in this place and over our lives and we submit ourselves to Him. We declare that we are here by legal right and that every enemy of the Lord Jesus Christ must be silent and leave this place immediately.

STARTER FILM – DVD

This Starter Film raises the questions, "Do you have an emotional satnav? And where is it taking you?"

It is designed to help participants start to recognize that our emotions can lead us down wrong paths. This is a key revelation for this generation as millennials tend to base decisions on how they feel.

And yet, our emotions are not a bad thing but are a gift from God. The second question starts to wrestle with this.

Remember that this is a time for discussion and there is no need to jump in and correct any view that might be expressed.

We so rarely take time to consider our emotions so this should be an interesting and enlightening Chat time!

KEY ONE – DVD

Rob opens up the discussion that was begun by the Starter Film. Millennials are prone to follow good experiences, decide how true something is by how it feels, and give up quickly when life gets tough. He challenges these things and the lie that when God feels distant, it means He must have left us.

He then looks at what emotions really are; that they are a God-given gift designed to indicate what's going on inside; and that negative emotions can be an indicator that you need to adjust your belief system – not give up and go another way.

Rob says that feeling depressed is a possible sign that our belief system is not in line with what God says is true. We don't want to convey the impression that all depression comes from faulty thinking – note the caveat on page 109 – but would recommend that anyone who struggles with depression, whatever they think causes it, pays particular attention to this section and ensures that it is not at the very least a contributory factor.

CHAT TIME ONE – PARTICIPANT'S GUIDE

Because the issue of making decisions based on how they feel is such a stumbling block to millennials' faith, it is the main focus of this session. It may be quite revelatory as they have probably never considered the concept that their emotions may be lying to them.

KEY TWO – DVD

David now looks at the reality that, although we cannot change our emotions overnight, we can change them over time with some effort. This is a real challenge to millennials who are not known for their perseverance! We cannot change our emotions directly. We change them by focusing on what we can change: our belief system.

He explains a key principle: that it is not life's events themselves that shape how we feel but our perception of them. We want to help participants understand that it is good to step back and evaluate their feelings rather than simply following them without thinking.

By looking at 1 Samuel 17, David shows the huge difference it makes when we look at our circumstances and take the whole of reality into account – including the truth that the all-powerful God is there in them, rather than leaving God out of the picture.

Finally, he looks at the three ways we process emotions: letting them out indiscriminately and exploding; burying them and ignoring them; or getting real with God and acknowledging how we feel, which is the only healthy way to process them.

He shows that handling our emotions better can be key in addressing issues of anger and aggression.

CHAT TIME TWO – PARTICIPANT'S GUIDE

This is a great opportunity for the group to further explore this issue of emotions and really recognize the need to measure what they see and feel against the truth of God's Word.

In the third question we look at Psalm 109. Many people are surprised at the level of raw honesty before God that David displays. We want them to understand that they need to develop an honest relationship with God if they are to grow. If they struggle with this, it can be helpful to remind them that He knows it all already and sharing how we feel is more for our benefit than His. It may also be good to remind them that God isn't there with a big stick expecting perfection – He is loving, patient, and delights in us – even when we are throwing a tantrum!

KEY THREE – DVD

Jess unpacks how lies we believe from our past can impact the way we feel and behave in the present. She shares about being assaulted by a serial sex attacker and how that experience left her feeling like a victim. She makes the point that it wasn't the attack itself that held her back in the long run so much as the lie the attack caused her to believe, which then dictated how she behaved.

This can be life-changing teaching for those who have suffered traumatic experiences or who have "messed up" in the past, and who now believe that they can't get free from those experiences. We want them to come to recognize that thinking this way is in itself a lie as no child of God is defined by their past, they are defined by Jesus' past. This can be particularly important with millennials because so many of them have started out without God, or have been so sucked into the world that they feel horrified and ashamed when they look back at the choices they made and the places they ended up.

She then looks at how we can get free from the things in the past which affect our future by making the choice to forgive, by looking at what happened again from the position we now have as children of God, and by discerning the lies that hold us back and dealing with them. This can be a real light bulb moment for the young adults who are hungry to serve God but who feel they are somehow held back by the past. It can be a special moment as they realize that they don't need to be held back by anything or anyone and can take hold of the freedom that Jesus has won for them and go on to make their lives count for eternity.

REFLECT

We would recommend breaking the group down into twos, partnering up with someone of the same gender.

Remind people to record lies that have come to light during this session on pages 190–191.

CONCLUDING REMARKS

Point out the Going Deeper section on page 117. It asks people to consider things in their past that they would rather forget.

Lots of people have things from the past that are holding them back. Encourage them that they will be able to start to deal with these issues in *The Steps To Freedom In Christ* and can have every expectation of walking free of them as they go on to renew their mind to the truth of God's Word. We will see how to do this in Session 9.

Let participants know what options there are if this session has brought up difficult issues for them that they would like to talk over with someone.

If anyone has significant issues from the past, we would recommend that you plan to take them through *The Steps To Freedom In Christ* in a personal appointment where they will have more time and more personal support. They can still take part in the group retreat first but tell them simply to do what they can there and not to worry at all if they get "stuck" or feel overwhelmed. Assure them that they can fully expect to move on from these things into a new phase of their life.

CLOSING PRAYER

Heavenly Father,
Thank You that it is for freedom that Jesus has set us free. Thank You that no one needs to be defined by their past but we are now defined by Jesus' past: His life, death, resurrection, and ascension to Your right hand. Father, we pray that You will give us peace about the things from the past that concern us and the resolve to deal with them once and for all when we go through *The Steps To Freedom In Christ*. Please see us home safely and give us a peaceful night's sleep.
In Jesus' name. Amen.

08 LEADER'S NOTES

Forgiving from the heart

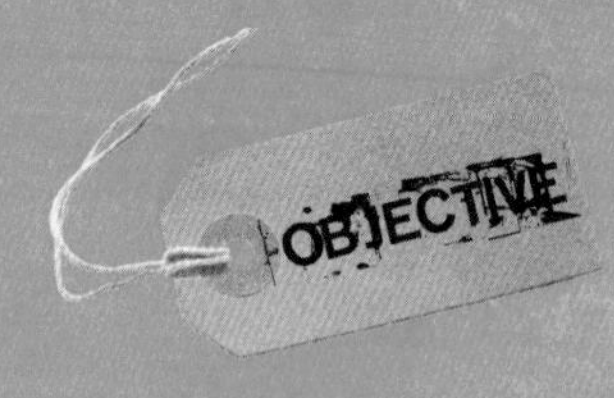

The notes for participants start on page 119.

In our experience, unforgiveness is the major issue that holds Christians back from being all that God created them to be. Freedom In Christ's teaching on forgiveness is the part that many people find most impactful. Our objective in this session is to help participants take hold of the fact that God commands us to forgive for our own wellbeing. We want them to understand, perhaps for the first time, what forgiveness is, what it isn't, and how to forgive from the heart.

The session focuses on the parable of the unforgiving servant in Matthew 18 (see page 123) and the key points are:

- We forgive because God commands us to, because He demonstrated forgiveness to us first, and for our own wellbeing.
- Unforgiveness allows the devil a foothold.
- We have to be intentional about who we forgive, even if we don't feel like it – it's a choice we make.
- Forgiveness is not forgetting or seeking revenge. It is choosing to hand the situation over to God and to trust Him to bring justice.
- By forgiving we make a choice to live with the consequences of what was done.
- Forgiveness is not so much an issue between us and the person that hurt us but is primarily between us and God.
- God is a loving Father to us who is intimately involved in our lives.

INTRODUCTION

The next time the group will meet after this session is for *The Steps To Freedom In Christ* retreat. Ensure that everyone knows where they need to be and when. Suggest that they bring a Bible and a pen or pencil with them. You will need to ensure that a copy of *The Steps To Freedom In Christ* is available for each person. We would suggest that you do not give these to people in advance of the day because some people might be tempted to start the process and it's better to do it all at one time. Refer people to page 133 for some information on the process and also to the extra film on *The Steps To Freedom In Christ* which is accessible via the *disciple* app.

In this session we will come across the last of our three "Truth Encounter" lists so, if you are using the postcards, make sure that you have the "My Father God" postcard available to distribute at the appropriate moment.

WORSHIP

Lead a short time of worship.

PRAYER

Dear Heavenly Father,
Thank You for Your grace and forgiveness, without which not one of us could stand before You. Please fill us with your Holy Spirit and teach us how to forgive so that we too can show grace and forgiveness to the people around us. We pray that You would saturate us with Your peace as we look at this crucial issue and lead us into the truth.
In Jesus' name. Amen.

DECLARATION

Hopefully participants are getting into the swing of asserting the authority they have in Christ through declarations. Encourage them to declare today's (on page 120) out loud. You might find it helpful to read it out a phrase at a time and get the group to repeat after you. Today's declaration is based on James 4:7 and reminds participants that they don't have to think every thought that comes into their mind but can take every thought captive.

I declare that my mind is my own and is to be a quiet place just for me and Jesus. I submit myself to God and I command – I don't suggest – I command every enemy of the Lord Jesus Christ to leave my presence immediately.

STARTER FILM – DVD

This Starter Film raises the question, "Can you really forgive?" and features an amazing testimony from Tamsin. She shares how she was able to show radical forgiveness after her husband hurt her deeply by having an affair with her best friend and leaving her with two very young children. It's a true, raw, and honest testimony that in some ways answers the question but leaves everyone in awe that forgiveness can be achieved even in the worst imaginable hurt and betrayal.

What happened to Tamsin will resonate deeply with some of the group who may come from broken families or have experienced a relationship break-up.

Although this time is not meant for teaching you might like to sum up the discussion very briefly by pointing out that forgiveness for the most serious issues is clearly possible and by reminding the group of the last session where we concluded that we are not defined by what happened to us in the past but can take hold of our freedom and move on.

KEY ONE – DVD

Rob unpacks the story of the unforgiving servant in Matthew 18. The aim of this section is to show that God commands us to forgive because He first forgave us and that if we don't forgive, we open ourselves up to spiritual attack which holds us back.

It can be a real shock to realize that forgiveness is about our own spiritual health – not just "doing the right thing" or "being a nice person". Millennials have a very strong sense of justice and so can think that forgiveness is achieved when justice is done. Understanding that we forgive so that we are no longer held back can be a real breakthrough moment.

CHAT TIME ONE – PARTICIPANT'S GUIDE

This Chat will help the group begin to reflect on how much they are forgiven – they don't need to share their past or hang out their dirty washing in public to do this.

Forgiveness starts with recognizing your own unpayable debt. For people who are new to Christianity or who ran away from God at some point, accepting that they have had a lot to be forgiven for is usually fairly straightforward. Sometimes those who have grown up in the church can find this harder, but they need to realize that even people who don't have a worldly past have still been forgiven a huge amount.

The second question helps participants understand that God's forgiveness of our sin was hugely costly. He sent His own Son to take our place and be executed as a common criminal in an excruciatingly painful, cruel, drawn-out process.

KEY TWO – DVD

In this session Jess unpacks what forgiveness really is and dispels the myth that it involves saying what happened was OK or didn't matter. She also makes clear that forgiveness isn't about forgetting or allowing sin to continue but it's about no longer seeking revenge and handing it all over to God, trusting that He will bring justice (Romans 12:19).

Understanding this principle will really help young adults who feel that forgiving someone somehow evades justice and should encourage them to take the step of forgiving those who hurt them.

CHAT TIME TWO – PARTICIPANT'S GUIDE

So many people misunderstand what forgiveness is so this is a really exciting session as they get to grips with it better.

In this session Jess talks about what a woman in an abusive relationship should do. Sometimes in the past, churches have been guilty of telling abused wives to submit to their husbands or, in other words, "Go home and be abused some more," – when in fact they needed to help them put an end to the abuse.

This may strike a nerve with people who have witnessed abuse or even suffered abuse themselves. You may even come across a situation where someone is in an abusive relationship of some sort and will need some help.

Make sure you understand your church's safeguarding policies and offer support as appropriate.

KEY THREE – DVD

In this section, David shares a powerful, true, and heartfelt testimony about his own childhood and how he eventually came to forgive his parents. Having demonstrated the power of forgiveness in his own life, he explains how all of us can choose to forgive from the heart.

This is a humbling and striking story, especially to a generation who so often have grown up in fragmented families. It's likely to speak very personally to some in the group as they process another powerful example of how forgiveness is simply a choice we need to make in order that we can be free.

David makes it clear that we can't wait until we feel like forgiving – because we probably never will – before he invites everyone to close their eyes and agree to forgive whoever God shows them. This can be a powerful moment as even those who thought they had no one to forgive are likely to be challenged by God to forgive someone. We encourage you to do whatever you can to ensure everyone engages with this. If people are stuck saying that they can't do it, remind them that it's their choice and they can.

David finishes this session with the third "Truth Encounter" list, "My Father God". Many of the group may have had difficult or dysfunctional relationships with their own fathers or may never have experienced a father in their lives. The problem is that it's all too easy for us to transfer how we feel about our earthly fathers onto God, which can negatively impact our relationship with God.

Do encourage them to read the list out loud with the DVD. Reading it aloud takes the truth so much deeper.

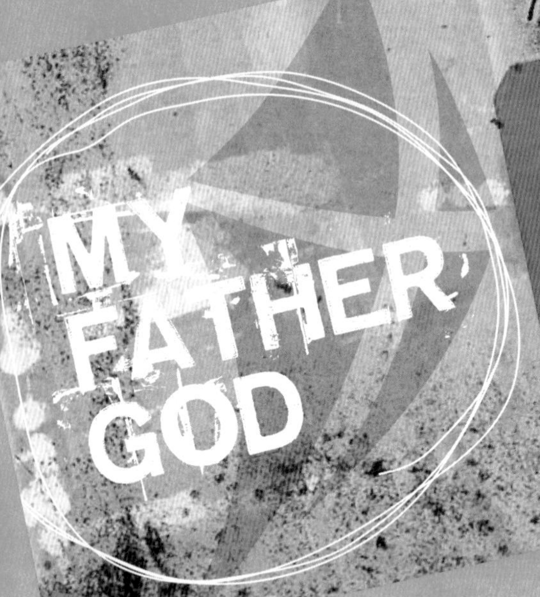

TRUTH ENCOUNTER

I renounce the lie that my Father God is distant or not interested in me.
I joyfully accept the truth that my Father God is intimate and involved [see Psalm 139:1–18].

I renounce the lie that my Father God is insensitive and uncaring.
I joyfully accept the truth that my Father God is kind and compassionate [see Psalm 103:8–14].

I renounce the lie that my Father God is strict and demanding.
I joyfully accept the truth that my Father God is accepting and filled with joy and love [see Romans 15:7; Zephaniah 3:17].

I renounce the lie that my Father God is passive and cold.
I joyfully accept the truth that my Father God is warm and affectionate [see Isaiah 40:11; Hosea 11:3–4].

I renounce the lie that my Father God is absent or too busy for me.
I joyfully accept the truth that my Father God is always with me and eager to be with me [see Hebrews 13:5; Jeremiah 31:20; Ezekiel 34:11–16].

I renounce the lie that my Father God is impatient, angry, or never satisfied with what I do.
I joyfully accept the truth that my Father God is patient and slow to anger and delights in those who put their hope in His unfailing love [see Exodus 34:6; 2 Peter 3:9; Psalm 147:11].

I renounce the lie that my Father God is mean, cruel, or abusive.
I joyfully accept the truth that my Father God loves me and is gentle and protective [see Jeremiah 31:3; Isaiah 42:3; Psalm 18:2].

I renounce the lie that my Father God is trying to take all the fun out of life.
I joyfully accept the truth that my Father God is trustworthy and wants to give me a full life; His will is good, perfect, and acceptable for me [see Lamentations 3:22–23; John 10:10; Romans 12:1–2].

I renounce the lie that my Father God is controlling or manipulative.
I joyfully accept the truth that my Father God is full of grace and mercy, and gives me freedom to fail [see Hebrews 4:15–16; Luke 15:11–16].

I renounce the lie that my Father God is condemning or unforgiving.
I joyfully accept the truth that my Father God is tender-hearted and forgiving; His heart and arms are always open to me [see Psalm 130:1–4; Luke 15:17–24].

I renounce the lie that my Father God is nit-picking or a demanding perfectionist.
I joyfully accept the truth that my Father God is committed to my growth and proud of me as His growing child [see Romans 8:28–29; Hebrews 12:5–11; 2 Corinthians 7:14].

I am the apple of His eye! [Deuteronomy 32:9–10].

REFLECT

This time is about looking more deeply at the "My Father God" truths and we suggest you break the group into twos or threes. These truths literally change lives so don't be tempted to rush this part and do encourage them to look into them further at home in their own time.

Ask them to take time to consider whether any lies have come to light during this session and to write these on pages 190–191.

Point out the Going Deeper section on page 132.

Struggling to relate to Father God is such a widespread problem that David has recorded an extra film for the app that is devoted solely to looking at who He really is.

People have found this session literally life-changing and we would encourage everyone to go through it, even those who have had good earthly fathers. They may well be amazed when they realize how loving their Father God is.

CONCLUDING REMARKS

Forgiveness is always a sensitive subject as it is tied to pain. Do encourage the group that *The Steps To Freedom In Christ* will be a real opportunity to resolve issues from the past.

Emphasize again that this is not to be missed and answer any questions they may have. Remind them that Jess has recorded an extra teaching film on *The Steps To Freedom In Christ* that they can watch via the app. She explains what it is and what it isn't, outlines how it works, and encourages everyone to go through it.

CLOSING PRAYER

Heavenly Father,

The truth of who You are and the level of grace and forgiveness You give us can be so hard to grasp. So often we misunderstand You. Please help us know You better and really grasp Your love, grace, and forgiveness. Please prepare us to go through *The Steps To Freedom In Christ* and prevent the enemy putting anything in the way of our getting there. We pray that it will be an incredible time of meeting with You and hearing from You. Please fill us with Your peace as we go from here and bless this night's sleep.

In Jesus' name. Amen.

LEADER'S NOTES

The Steps To Freedom In Christ

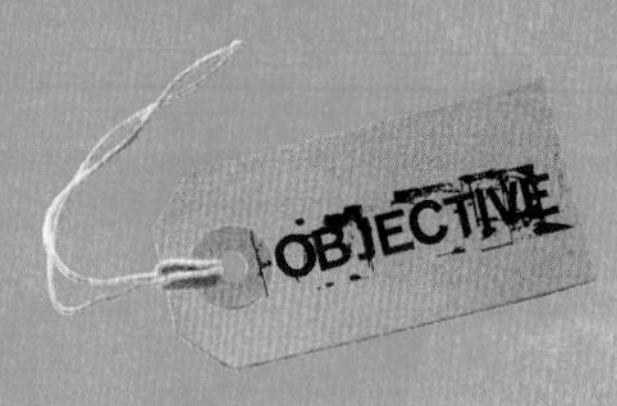

This section of the Leader's Guide is designed to help you understand the ministry component of *disciple*, *The Steps To Freedom In Christ*, and how to lead it. Much of it has been adapted with permission from *The Freedom In Christ Course* by Neil T. Anderson and Steve Goss. Please read it in conjunction with the introductory section on pages 222–223.

The Steps process is a crucial part of the course. Without it, you will find that people may appreciate the great truth they have heard, but they will probably not be able to put it into practice.

This section covers the following:

1. What is *The Steps To Freedom In Christ*?
2. Running an "Away Day".
3. Running an individual "Freedom Appointment".
4. Understanding why *The Steps To Freedom In Christ* works.

1. WHAT IS *THE STEPS TO FREEDOM IN CHRIST*?

The Steps To Freedom In Christ is a structured process of prayers and declarations written by Neil T. Anderson, the Founder of Freedom In Christ Ministries. It has been used by millions of Christians around the world. Each participant will need a copy of *The Steps To Freedom In Christ* booklet so ensure you order these in advance.

The process is based on James 4:7 which says, "Submit yourselves, then, to God. Resist the devil, and he will flee from you." It is an opportunity for participants to spend time with God and lay everything on the table before Him, asking Him to show them through the Holy Spirit where there are footholds of the enemy in their lives.

Each participant is in control of the process: it is between them and God. No one else is hearing from God on their behalf or telling them what issues they need to deal with. They ask the Holy Spirit to show them what they need to deal with and He does. They then take the responsibility to remove the footholds through repentance and renouncing sin. There are structured prayers which provide a framework to do this.

Renouncing something means giving up a claim to it. We are making a definite decision before God to let go of ungodly commitments, pledges, vows, pacts, and beliefs.

When it's all over, participants will tell the enemy to leave their presence and he has no option but to flee from them because they have submitted to God and are now actively resisting him. They then have the responsibility to stand firm in the freedom they have won by committing themselves to renew their minds to the truth in God's Word.

The process is led by the Holy Spirit and, because the person seeking freedom is in control, it is gentle, kind, and generally undramatic. But the changes it brings about can be far-reaching and hugely significant.

There are seven steps. They serve as a sort of inventory of aspects of our lives.

Step 1 is about false guidance and participation in the occult and false religions. This covers fake spiritual stuff that the world tells us can replace God but which gets in the way of our relationship with Him.

Step 2 is about deception, which is the major strategy of the enemy, the father of lies. This is an important step in taking hold of freedom, by sorting out the lies and choosing truth instead.

Step 3 deals with unforgiveness, which, in our experience, is the number one way that Satan neutralizes Christians.

Step 4 covers rebellion, which can be a particularly difficult issue for the millennial generation who struggle with the concept of godly submission, particularly in marriage.

Step 5 is where participants are invited to renounce pride in all its forms, including prejudice and bigotry.

Step 6 deals with habitual sins that have become strongholds – those "sin-confess-sin-confess cycles" that we have all fallen prey to at some time or another. Sexual sins are dealt with here too.

Step 7 is about issues from previous generations that may be affecting us. Participants are invited to renounce the sins of our ancestors. It is not that we are guilty of our parents' sins, but because they sinned we live with the consequence of their sins. In the same way that all human beings are the genetic product of their natural parents and are predisposed to their parents' strengths and weaknesses, we are their spiritual product and can be affected by patterns of behaviour and sin.

Participants should be given an opportunity to go through *The Steps To Freedom In Christ* between Sessions 8 and 9 of *disciple*.

The process runs under the auspices of your church and it's important to make sure that you understand the relevant legal aspects to do with safeguarding and reporting. Ensure your church's protection policies are up-to-date and that you know how they work. Make sure that in the case of minors a parent/guardian gives permission.

There are two different approaches you can take. You can either go through the Steps as a group on an "Away Day" or you can give each individual their own personal "freedom appointment".

2. RUNNING AN "AWAY DAY"

Let's look first at the Away Day approach where you take your whole group through the process at the same time. The advantage of an Away Day is that you can get a lot of people through the Steps at one time. There are leaders on hand to help if people get stuck. However, some will have too much "stuff" to process and will need to have their own one-to-one appointment following a group Away Day.

The Away Day can include Session 8 of *disciple*, the session on forgiveness. You would insert it immediately before the forgiveness step where people actually do the forgiving they need to do.

It is recommended that you hold the Away Day in pleasant surroundings, away from your church if possible. Aim to provide lunch or make sure that people bring packed lunches – it is recommended that you maintain a quiet atmosphere over lunchtime and suggest that people remain on the premises. You will find a suggested timetable on page 318.

The room you use should be large enough for participants to have some degree of privacy. They will say the opening prayers together but will then spread out so that they spend time just between them and God. It's important that people understand, in fact, that this is not some kind of "group confessional" where they are expected to share in front of others. They will in fact spread out and find a quiet space where they can speak to God quietly. It can be helpful to have some music playing in the background during the Steps so that people can pray out loud without feeling that others are listening. Instrumental music works best as it is less distracting.

Each participant will need a copy of *The Steps To Freedom In Christ* booklet, their *disciple* Participant's Guide, and a pencil. The group will be praying several prayers together out loud. Then they will spend some time alone with God. Nobody will be embarrassed or asked to share anything with the group or another person. It is solely an encounter with God. Explain to the group that some will get in touch with real pain, and tears are understandable and acceptable.

People will at times benefit from individual attention during the Steps that they find difficult (usually Steps 1, 3, and 6). Plan to have a reasonable number of people whose role is to walk around and help those who are struggling (one for every ten people would be a good starting point). These should be mature Christians who have had their own freedom appointment and are well acquainted with the principles that are taught in *disciple*.

Some people will have very little to deal with on some Steps, whereas others may have a lot. Suggest that those who do not have much on a particular Step spend time praying for those who do: that the Holy Spirit will reveal everything that needs to be revealed; and that Satan's attempts to interfere in the process will be ineffective. If people have too much to deal with in the time available, reassure them that this is not a one-off opportunity and that they will be able to catch up in due course, ideally by having their own personal freedom appointment.

Most use the Steps DVD to guide people through the process because it does most of the work for you and stops automatically in the right place. You will obviously need a TV monitor or projector that everyone can see, and a DVD player. Start with prayer, and then explain how the session will work. Start the Steps DVD, which begins with some explanatory remarks about the Steps and the process they will be going through. Each Step will be explained and begun with group prayer. When the prayer and final instructions for the Step have finished, the DVD pauses automatically. Wait until everybody has finished that Step or that part of the Step and has come back together and then press "Play".

Suggested Timetable For An Away Day

This is a suggested timetable for taking a group through Session 8 and *The Steps To Freedom In Christ* on an Away Day:

9.45	Welcome and worship
10.10	Introduction (10 minutes) Step 1 (30 minutes) Step 2 (30 minutes)
11.20	Break
11.35	*disciple* Session 8: Forgiving From The Heart (DVD sections only – no discussion)
12.10	Step 3 (40 minutes – but can expand into lunchtime if required)
13.00	Lunch Break
14.00	Step 4 (15 minutes) Step 5 (15 minutes) Step 6 (40 minutes) Step 7 (10 minutes)
15.20	Break
15.40	Worship
16.00	Concluding remarks
16.15	Finish

3. RUNNING AN INDIVIDUAL "FREEDOM APPOINTMENT"

An individual appointment typically takes three to five hours. It is more personal and is the ideal. People tend to go much deeper when they are confessing out loud to God in front of someone else.

If you can manage it, our advice is to go for the individual appointment approach for everyone. You will find that it doesn't take as long as you might think to build up a team who can help others through. Leading someone through an appointment doesn't require any particular expertise. You are not there to "fix" someone, simply to encourage.

In an individual appointment there are typically three people in attendance: the person seeking freedom; the person facilitating the process whom we call the "Encourager"; and a prayer partner who is there to support the process in prayer.

The qualifications of an Encourager are that they have had their own personal appointment, they understand that it's Jesus who sets people free, they rely on the Holy Spirit, and they have a good grasp of truth so that they can help identify lies that the freedom seeker may believe.

Freedom In Christ can usually arrange for up to two of your leaders to have a personal appointment to enable your church to see how it works and get started. That's just so that you can see best practice. It doesn't then take long for you to build a team. It's also perfectly OK simply to get started by taking each other through the process. It is straightforward and self-explanatory.

The prayer partner will quietly pray throughout the process. Often they will share insights and encouragements. They too will be looking out for any lies that the freedom seeker has been believing. Typically a prayer partner is learning to become an Encourager.

1. Start By Gathering Background Information

Choose a comfortable room and allow for several hours should the case be difficult. Have a box of tissues available, and some water.

We strongly recommend that you get the freedom seeker to complete some kind of statement of understanding that lays out the basis of the appointment. It would say, for example, that this is not a counselling appointment but is simply one Christian helping another, that if anything comes to light that must legally be reported to the authorities then it will be, and that participants are there voluntarily. Freedom In Christ Ministries can supply suggested text for you to adapt.

We also suggest that participants on an individual appointment complete a Confidential Personal Inventory before the appointment, in which they give some personal background information. Again, Freedom In Christ Ministries can supply text that you can use as a basis.

First, get a brief history of their family. What were the religious experiences of their parents or grandparents? Were they involved in the occult or a counterfeit religion? Was there harmony in the home? Have there been any divorces or affairs in the family history? Dysfunctional families breed false beliefs. For example, many children wrongly blame themselves for their parents' divorce. Others harbour bitterness toward their parents for years because of something that happened in their home.

You will want to know if their family has any history of alcoholism, drug abuse, sexual addiction, or mental illness. What type of exercise and eating habits characterized the family? What was the moral climate in the home? Ask them to share their early childhood and school experiences.

Note that you are not trying to resolve anything by hearing their personal and family history. The purpose is to understand what happened to them and what may have caused them to have certain beliefs. The intimate details will come out when you take them through the Steps.

The Confidential Personal Inventory also provides important information concerning their physical, mental, emotional, and spiritual life.

2. Lead Them Through The Steps

The primary focus of the Steps is their relationship with God. The process is different from most counselling approaches, because the one who is praying is the one who needs the help, and they are praying to the only One who can help them.

Explain to the freedom seeker what they are doing and why they are doing it. Try to go through all seven steps in one session. They may not need every step but you want to be thorough for their sake. Have them read every prayer and doctrinal affirmation aloud. Hopefully they will share any mental opposition or physical discomfort. When they do, thank them for sharing it with you. Once it is acknowledged, simply go on. In most cases there is very little opposition. Spiritual opposition usually shows up only in the first two steps.

Unforgiveness (Step 3) is the most critical Step. Every person has at least one person and usually several people to forgive. Unforgiveness affords the biggest door to the Church for Satan. If we can't help a person forgive from the heart, we can't help them be free from their past.

When they pray and ask God whom they need to forgive, rest assured that God does reveal names to their mind. If they say, "Well there is no one," then respond by saying, "Would you just share the names that are coming to your mind right now?" Inevitably, several names will surface, and you should record them on a sheet of paper. It is not uncommon for freedom-seekers to have names come to mind that surprise them. And it is not uncommon for them to recall forgotten painful memories while in the process of forgiving.

Explain what forgiveness is and how to do it. The key issues are highlighted in the Steps book. Then hand the list back to them and ask if they would be willing to forgive those people for their own sake. Forgiving others is primarily an issue between them and their Heavenly Father. Reconciliation may or may not follow.

Very little opposition occurs during Steps 4 to 6. In Step 6, deal with sexual sins separately. It is amazing how much sex plays a part in human bondage and that is particularly true for many millennials. There are several prayers that they could pray in Step 6 for specific issues. Ask if any are pertinent to them.

In most cases complete freedom isn't realized until after the final declaration and prayer in Step 7. When they have finished, ask the freedom seeker to sit comfortably and close their eyes. Then ask, "What do you hear in your mind? Is it quiet?" After a pause they usually respond with a relieved smile and say, "Nothing. It's finally quiet in my mind." If they had difficulty reading the statements of truth in Step 2, have them read it again. They can hardly believe the ease with which they can now read and understand the truth. The whole demeanour of many freedom seekers often changes so dramatically that you may want them to look at themselves in a mirror.

3. Keep Pointing People Towards Truth

Most people caught in a spiritual conflict have a distorted concept of God and themselves, and it will help you if you can determine what those false beliefs are. Listen carefully to what is said. It may be helpful in some cases to review from previous sessions the truth about God and who we are in Christ. Defeated Christians don't know who they are in Christ, or understand what it means to be a child of God. Consequently, they question their salvation. Many think they are different from other people. The Christian life doesn't seem to work for them as it does for others. Some fear a mental breakdown and are filled with anxiety. Almost all feel unloved, worthless, and rejected. They have tried everything they can think of to improve their self-image, but nothing works. Some even suspect that their problem is spiritual, but they don't know how to resolve their conflicts.

Defeated Christians often have a distorted concept of the two kingdoms. They think they are caught between two equal but opposite powers. Bad old Satan is on one side, good old God is on the other, and poor old me is caught in the middle. That of course is not true, and they are defeated if that is what they believe. The truth is; God is omnipresent, omnipotent, and omniscient. Satan is a defeated foe and we are alive in Christ, and seated with Him at the right hand of the Father, the ultimate seat of power and authority in the universe.

One of the key things people can take from the Steps is an understanding of what lies they are prone to believe. In Session 9 of *disciple* they will learn about "stronghold-busting" a structured way to renew their mind.

4. When There Is A Major Battle For The Mind
The Steps process is for every Christian, not just those with obvious problems. However, it can help those with deeper issues too.

To some people Satan seems to be more present, real, and powerful than God. This type of person faces a major battle for their mind and usually hears opposing arguments in their head. They are constantly confronted with lies, told to get out of the freedom appointment, or threatened with harm or embarrassment.

Such mental interference is not uncommon. Explain that thoughts are like planes asking for permission to land and they are like the air traffic controller. They don't have to think and act on every thought that appears in their minds but can decide which are permitted to land and which need to be turned away. If they don't lose control in their minds, then you will not lose control in the freedom appointment. In one sense it doesn't matter whether the negative or condemning thoughts are coming from a loudspeaker on the wall, from their own memory, or from the pit of hell. The only way those thoughts can have any control over them is if they believe them. To help them maintain mental control, ask them regularly to share what is going on in their minds. You want them to bring those deceptive thoughts into the light. As soon as the lie is exposed, the power is broken.

They may be reluctant to share with you for two reasons. First, if they sense that you won't believe them, they won't tell you. If the freedom-seeker is hearing voices, secular counsellors and many Christian counsellors would not consider the voices to be demonic. They will be given a psychological label and a prescription for medication. Realizing this, the troubled person may share what has happened to them, but would be very reluctant to share the mental battle that is going on inside. Second, if they are hearing demonic voices, those voices can be very intimidating. They could be threatening harm to the freedom seeker, the Encourager, or family and friends of the freedom seeker.

Watch their eyes very carefully. If they start to become dizzy or glassy-eyed, or start looking around the room, stop what you are doing and ask them to share what is going on inside. If you aren't paying attention, you could lose control of the session. If they are really struggling mentally, encourage them to get up and go for a walk. You want them to know that they have a choice and that they can exercise their will.

Highly subjective people are the hardest to help because they have never really assumed responsibility for their own thoughts; they have a thought and they act on it. They don't seem to realize they have a will or can say no to negative thoughts. Instruct them by saying, "If you have a thought, don't just do what it says. Share it with me." Help them understand that not every thought that comes into their mind is necessarily their own. It is revolutionary for some people to understand that their mind is their own and that they can decide which thoughts they will allow to "come in to land" and which to turn away.

To help maintain control, the Steps begin with a very specific prayer and declaration. If they have made a declaration of faith in God, Satan cannot harm them, because he has no authority over them.

We recommend that you don't touch the person during a freedom appointment – if the person has been abused in the past, they may feel as if they have been violated. People still under demonic oppression will recoil, and move away from you. After they are free, however, just the opposite happens. They move towards you. Opposite spirits repel, but the Holy Spirit unites.

Never try to restrain anyone physically, because the weapons of our warfare are not of the flesh (2 Corinthians 10:3–4). If they run out of the room, let them go. Wait and pray, and invariably they come back, usually within five minutes. We should never violate their mind or try to control them. They are free to leave or stay.

If the person you are trying to help has been actively involved in Satanism, be prepared for major opposition. Step 1 contains a page of special renunciations for those who have worshipped Satan or been subjected to satanic ritual abuse. Everything they do is an antithesis of Christianity, because Satan is the Antichrist. It could take you several hours to work through those renunciations.

4. UNDERSTANDING WHY *THE STEPS TO FREEDOM IN CHRIST* WORKS

Here are some key characteristics of the Steps process:

- The method doesn't require experts – it can be conducted by any reasonably mature Christian who is walking in freedom – so is easily transferable.
- It produces lasting results because the freedom seekers are the ones making the decisions and assuming personal responsibility, rather than a pastor or counsellor doing it for them.
- It doesn't bypass the person's mind.
- The focus is on Christ and repentance. The real issue isn't Satan, it is God and our walk with Him. The seven Steps are seven issues that are critical between ourselves and God.

There are three key principles that it is helpful to understand as you prepare to lead people through *The Steps To Freedom In Christ*.

1. This Is A Truth Encounter Not A Power Encounter

Before the cross, Satan was not a defeated foe, and the Church was not yet in existence. Believers were not born again. In that environment it would take someone with specially endowed authority from God to confront the demonic. Jesus was one such person and clearly demonstrated His authority and power over the kingdom of darkness. He also conferred this onto the twelve disciples (Luke 9:1), and then the seventy-two (Luke 10).

We are now living in a completely different spiritual environment. Now every believer is a new creation in Christ and seated with Him in the heavenly realms.

Casting out demons is no longer the responsibility of an outside agent. Every Christian has the same standing in Christ, and we can't confess, repent, believe, renounce, forgive, or assume any responsibility for another person. That is why there are no instructions for casting out demons in the New Testament letters.

Some Christians have adopted their methodology from the Gospels, which, of course, deal with the spiritual environment that existed before the cross. They may attempt to call up demons, get their name and rank, and cast them out. With this approach, the pastor or counsellor is the deliverer and he or she is getting information from a demon. We should never believe demons, however, because they are all liars: "When he lies, he speaks his native language, for he is a liar and the father of lies." (John 8:44)

If you were successful in casting a demon out of someone without his or her involvement, what is to keep the demon from coming back when you leave? Unless the individual assumes responsibility for their own freedom, they may end up being freed from one spirit only to be occupied by seven others who were worse than the first (Matthew 12:43–45).

The New Testament letters (which were written in the spiritual environment that existed after the cross) teach a different approach when the person seeking freedom is a Christian. First, the deliverer is Christ and He has already come. Second, we should get our information from the Word of God and the Holy Spirit who will lead us into all truth and that truth will set us free. If we try to resist the devil without first submitting to God, the result will be a dogfight. On the other hand, we can submit to God without resisting the devil and stay in bondage, which sadly is where many Christians find themselves. They have come to Christ but have never been taught how to close the door to the enemy's influence in their lives through genuine repentance.

In order for a Christian to be set free, there is no need for a power encounter. The only power encounter needed took place two thousand years ago when Jesus completely disarmed Satan (Colossians 2:15). There is not a verse in the Bible that instructs us to pursue power because believers already have all the power they need in Christ (Ephesians 1:18–19).

Satan's power is in his ability to deceive. His power is only effective in the dark. However, all the darkness in the world cannot extinguish the light of one candle. Knowing the truth is what will set us free. Christians are to pursue the truth because they already have the power and authority to do His will. Truth is what makes an encounter with Satan effective because his primary strategy is deception.

Satan fears detection more than anything else. Whenever the light of truth comes on, he and his demons head for the shadows like cockroaches. Demons are afraid of God and of being exposed to the truth.

2. Individuals Must Assume Responsibility

God has set the world up in a certain way. He has given us certain responsibilities while keeping others for Himself. Nothing will interfere more in the process of someone growing to maturity if we try to play God's role in their life.

The Steps To Freedom In Christ process follows the principles in this verse: "Submit... to God. Resist the devil, and he will flee from you." (James 4:7) Who is the one who has to do the submitting and resisting? The person seeking freedom.

Most defeated Christians are in effect hoping that God will change His ways to accommodate them. They want God or you to assume their responsibility. God will not do that and we cannot do it. We can't submit, resist, repent, forgive, or believe the truth for anyone else.

James 5:13–16 gives clear instructions on who is to do what if someone is in trouble or sick. Note that it is the struggling person that needs to take the initiative. The one who is in trouble is to pray. The one who is sick is to call the elders of the church.

Note also the order that things are to be done in verse 16: "Therefore confess your sins to each other and pray for each other so that you may be healed. The prayer of a righteous man is powerful and effective."

Confession comes first. If you prayed for someone and you later discovered that they were locked into sins of pride, bitterness, and rebellion, would you be surprised if God did not answer your prayer? Of course not. "If I had cherished sin in my heart, the Lord would not have listened." (Psalm 66:18) It's essential that they first take on board their responsibility to confess their sins.

Confession is simply agreeing with God – being honest. All secular counsellors will tell you that healing starts with honesty – facing up to the truth.

They also need to repent, which includes actively shutting the door on the sin and taking back any ground given to the enemy. Again, we cannot do that for them.

We can take great encouragement from this: it's not our responsibility to work out what the problem is and "fix" someone. Our role is to encourage them to ask the Lord to reveal any issues to them and to point them towards truth.

We can help them, however, and Paul indicates how in 2 Timothy 2:24–26:

> And the Lord's servant must not be quarrelsome; but must be kind to everyone, able to teach, not resentful. Opponents must be gently instructed, in the hope that God will grant them repentance leading them to a knowledge of the truth, and that they will come to their senses and escape from the trap of the devil, who has taken them captive to do his will.

This passage teaches that truth sets people free and that God is the One who grants repentance. Only God can bind up the broken-hearted and set the captive free. God does, however, work through His servants who are dependent upon Him. But our role is to point them always to the Wonderful Counsellor rather than try and "fix" them ourselves.

According to 2 Timothy 2:24–26, our primary qualification as the one leading is to be "the Lord's servant". To be an instrument in God's hand we have to be totally dependent upon Him. Beyond that requirement, the Lord's servant must be kind, patient, gentle, and able to teach. In other words, we need to know and speak the truth in love, because truth sets us free. Christians are not in bondage to past traumas. They are in bondage to the lies they came to believe as a result of past traumas. We can help them by pointing to the truth.

3. We Are Teaching A Way Of Life

The Steps To Freedom In Christ doesn't set anyone free! Who sets them free is Christ. What sets them free is their response to Him in repentance and faith.

The last thing we want is for people to think they have "done" *The Steps To Freedom In Christ* as if it were a one-off experience or a box that they have now ticked. The objective is to help them become fruitful disciples of Jesus and, in order to do that, we don't want to give them a one-off experience of freedom, but equip them for the future.

If people go through the Steps in a group on an Away Day, encourage them also to have their own individual freedom appointment where they speak out loud in front of another person. This could be as simple as doing it together with a trusted friend. Encourage them to revisit the process on a regular basis, perhaps annually. They won't, of course, need to deal with issues again if they have not fallen back into that particular sin but it's amazing what we can accumulate in a year.

Note too that there is a great difference between freedom and maturity. Session 9 of *disciple* teaches more about this. Suffice to say for now that taking hold of freedom through the Steps process is no guarantee that people will remain in that freedom. They will now, however, be able to make a free choice to renew their mind (the only way to be transformed – see Romans 12:2), perhaps for the first time using the stronghold-busting tool outlined in Session 9 of *disciple*.

09 LEADER'S NOTES

Walking into the next chapter

The notes for participants start on page 135.

We hope that participants have by now understood their amazing new identity in Christ, have recognized how the world, the flesh, and the devil try to feed them lies, and have taken back any ground given to the enemy through unresolved personal and spiritual conflicts. Along the way we hope they have become aware of beliefs they have held that do not line up with God's Word and have listed these on pages 190–191. The stage is now set for the rest of their lives!

We have talked a lot about how our minds are the battleground for the struggle between the Spirit of truth and the father of lies, how we need to take every thought captive and how it is by renewing our minds that we are transformed. In this session we want to give participants a practical way of renewing their minds that we hope will become a way of life for them. We also want to help them understand that God's goal for the rest of their lives is that they become more and more like Jesus in character. As they head towards this goal, they will find that their actions automatically become more and more like His. The key points are:

- As Christians, we are meant to keep growing to maturity but it's not inevitable that we will.
- Freedom and maturity are not the same thing but you can't become mature unless you have first taken hold of your freedom.
- It is by renewing our minds to the truth of God's Word that we will be transformed but this takes time and effort.
- Our story is now headed in a new direction, towards a new goal.
- God is primarily interested in what you are *like* not what you *do* – because what you do flows from who you are.
- God's goal for our lives is that we become more and more like Jesus and we need to make sure our goals are in line with His.
- We may have developed other good goals but if they depend on people or circumstances outside our control, they set us up for problems.

INTRODUCTION

Ask people to share briefly how they got on with *The Steps To Freedom In Christ*. Did they find it helpful? Did anything surprising happen? Did they sense God speaking?

Participants may now feel they have "been there, done that" when it comes to the Steps – guard against the impression that this is a one-off event. Emphasize that, just as you service your car on a regular basis, it's good to get into the habit of going through this amazing spiritual check-up on a regular basis. We recommend going through the Steps at least annually. You can, of course, dip into it at any time in the event that you become aware of a particular issue that needs dealing with.

WORSHIP

Lead a short time of worship.

PRAYER

Dear Heavenly Father,
Thank You for taking us through *The Steps To Freedom In Christ* and leading us into the freedom that Jesus won for us. It's wonderful to be free but we also want to grow. And we want our lives to make a real impact for You. Thank You that you have more to teach us. Please fill us with your Holy Spirit and show us how to become more and more like Jesus so that we will increasingly find ourselves doing the things that Jesus did.
We pray in His wonderful name. Amen.

DECLARATION

Participants will have had lots of practice making declarations during the Steps so hopefully won't need huge encouragement to declare today's declaration on page 136 loudly and boldly!

In Jesus' name we declare that God is sovereign in this place and over our lives and that we are here by legal right. And so we tell every enemy of the Lord Jesus Christ to be silent and leave this place immediately. You will not stop the will of God being done in this group.

STARTER FILM – DVD

This Starter Film raises the question, "How can you really change?"

Although participants have taken hold of their freedom and are now free if they did real business with God when they went through *The Steps To Freedom In Christ*, they still have the old fleshly thought patterns or "strongholds". The Steps is just the start. Real change comes through renewing our minds. Often after the Steps people think that's it, it's all done. So it can be a bit of a wake-up call to realize that they now have some work to do to keep walking in freedom.

The film sets the scene for the process of "stronghold-busting" that we will introduce during this session. Stronghold-busting is an amazingly powerful tool to renew our minds but it takes time and effort. This is a particular challenge to the millennial generation who find perseverance difficult.

At the end of the discussion, encourage the group that this session will give them the tools they need to be radically transformed by Jesus!

KEY ONE – DVD

Jess kicks this teaching off by looking at Hebrews 12:1–2 and 5:14 and discussing how we now need to run the race with perseverance. She notes that freedom is a great platform to grow from but is not the same thing as maturity.

She then looks at Romans 12:2 and explains the stronghold-busting process, a key tool that people will take away from *disciple*. Using the example of compulsive gambling, she shows how you can use it to dismantle any stronghold but it takes time and effort.

CHAT TIME ONE – PARTICIPANT'S GUIDE

We cannot emphasize enough how significant stronghold-busting can be if people take hold of it and use it. It is one of the most important things that participants can take from the course and for many something that they will use for the rest of their lives. This Chat is a crucial opportunity for people to start to get to grips with it and we recommend allowing at least 30 minutes.

Take up to 5 minutes at the start to run people through the notes on pages 140–144 and point out the space for them to write their own stronghold-busters on pages 146–151. Demonstrate briefly the Stronghold-Busting section of the app where participants can develop stronghold-busters and set up daily reminders to use them. If you have your own experience of stronghold-busting it would be fantastic for you to share it briefly during this time. Emphasize perhaps how hard it was to persevere to start with but what a difference it made in the end.

The millennial generation struggles to commit to doing stronghold-busters, preferring to look for a "quick fix". Being feelings-driven and experiential they tend to get too quickly disheartened when they don't instantly see the fruit. We want the group to understand that if they commit to doing a stronghold-buster and persevere, they will get free from any stronghold that they want to deal with. Reiterate this as may times as you feel you can during this Chat!

It's now time for the group to start to develop their own stronghold-buster. People can work on their own or in pairs. Each person should select the most significant lie they realize they have believed. Hopefully they have been recording these on pages 190–191.

You may need to wander around and help people identify appropriate truths from the Bible if they get stuck. Many of the truths they will need are already on the "Truth Encounter" lists from sessions 2, 3, and 8 that they can access in the Participant's Guide, on the app or on the postcards. Very often the root lie boils down to not feeling secure, significant or accepted so the "Who I Am In Jesus" list is a great starting place.

In our experience, if participants don't get their first stronghold-buster constructed and started now, the odds of their following through with it diminish sharply. Extend this time as much as is practical or offer help at the end or before the next session for anyone who doesn't manage to finish.

Finally, suggest that people pair up to encourage each other to do their stronghold-buster every day, reminding them that to start with it is likely to feel like a total waste of time. They could call or message each other daily to see how each other is doing and to offer encouragement to keep going.

KEY TWO – DVD

In this section David makes it clear that God has given us everything we need to live a godly life (2 Peter 1:3) and unpacks what a godly goal looks like. He concludes that God is primarily concerned with our character and that the best goal we can have is simply to become more and more like Jesus in character. Each one of us can do that.

This is very liberating for young adults who have been subliminally programmed to achieve and be the best. Throughout school they are driven to try and achieve the highest grades possible; society says that to have the car and the house and the great job is what will make you a success. How liberating it is to have the light bulb moment when you realize that what you are *like* is far more important than what you *do*! Because what you do will come from who you are.

David then talks about our goals in life. Note that there is a useful outline of the logic of his argument on page 155. David points out that when our goals are uncertain we become anxious, when they are blocked we feel angry, and when they feel unachievable we can become depressed.

Please do note that we are not suggesting that depression is simply an issue of having a goal that seems impossible. This is just one possible cause. You will recall our explanatory note on page 109 and might like to refer people to it. Depression is a complex issue that needs a holistic approach to address it. Whilst it's true to say that addressing ungodly goals has seen many people set free from the symptoms of depression, it can have many roots including chemical and hormonal issues. If people suffer from depression, going through *The Steps To Freedom In Christ*, identifying faulty beliefs and renewing the mind and downgrading ungodly goals is a great starting point. However, if it persists they would be well advised to see a medical doctor.

CHAT TIME TWO – PARTICIPANT'S GUIDE

This Chat time will give the group the opportunity to look at the goals that they have knowingly or unknowingly set themselves. Remember that a goal (in the way we are using the term here) is something that seems so important to them that their very sense of success or failure as a person depends on whether or not they achieve it.

It's not about giving up on dreams – it's about downgrading unhelpful goals to desires so that we don't feel devastated if we don't achieve it.

It's likely to be an interesting and lively chat when you consider how countercultural these concepts are.

KEY THREE – DVD

Millennials don't like "religion" so in this session Rob squashes any ideas that being a disciple is about religion and affirms that it's about getting to know Jesus better – our walk with God is rooted in our relationship with Him.

Because of their dislike of religion, millennials can tend to turn away from the organized church. At the end of this session Rob points out that we are all part of the body of Christ and we need to be plugged into a Christian community so that we can love and support each other on this journey.

He finishes this with a prayer in which people are invited to commit themselves to be part of the body of Christ rather than just lone rangers. This can be a real challenge and some may not want to pray it at first. Please don't put pressure on them. Some people have had a difficult past with the church and getting them to actively engage with a fellowship of believers may be a process. Instead, simply pray over the coming days that they will hear God's call to connect with the body of Christ.

REFLECT

We suggest that people spend some time on their own with God for this Reflect time.

It is about allowing some space for the truth to sink in that Christianity isn't about religion and is not a list of rules, even if some people reduce it to those things. The revelation that it's about a day-by-day relationship with a real person – who just happens to be the Creator Himself! – is amazing.

It also challenges any who are not committed to a fellowship of believers that they are part of the body of Christ. If you have any participants on your course who fall into that category, don't automatically assume that your church is the best place for them. Come armed with research about other churches in your area of all types. Don't assume, for example, that all young adults want loud modern music. Some millennials really meet God amongst liturgy and more traditional expressions of worship.

CONCLUDING REMARKS

As you close, point out the Going Deeper section in the Participant's Guide and end with another encouragement to get stuck into their new stronghold-buster!

CLOSING PRAYER

Heavenly Father,
Thank You that You promise to finish the work You have started in us and that in the meantime You are proud of us as your growing children and delight in us just as we are. Thank You that we can all grow and become more and more like Jesus in character as we get to know You better. As we go from here, please help us to persevere with our stronghold-busters even when our feelings and our enemies tell us it's pointless. Thank You that You promise us transformation as we choose to renew our minds and that is what we want.
We pray in Jesus' name. Amen.

10 LEADER'S NOTES

Action story

The notes for participants start on page 161.

It's been quite a journey and here we are at the last session of *disciple*! All we have done so far has been leading up to this point. We have helped people grasp who they are in Jesus, what they have in Him, how to deal with issues that hold them back, and how to be transformed through the renewal of their mind.

The objective of all this is not just so that they can resolve past issues and feel good about themselves. It's so that they can take their place in God's incredible plans and do the works that He has prepared for them. It's about the rest of their lives being surrendered to God. It's about going out in the power of the Holy Spirit together as part of the body of Christ and making a real difference.

The message that this session has for every child of God is:

- God chose <u>you</u>!
- You are a minister of reconciliation.
- You are Jesus' ambassador.
- You are in Christ but Christ is also in you.
- You have freedom to choose how your story goes on from here – do you want to build treasure in heaven or on earth?
- What you do will be tested in the end but God will love you whether or not you use your life to make an eternal difference.
- We share Jesus' mandate to proclaim the good news and bring justice, righteousness, and freedom.
- We have a choice – God doesn't tell us what we have to do but He invites us to join Him.
- You can be an ambassador right where God has already placed you.

INTRODUCTION

Start by asking people how their stronghold-busters are going. Note, however, that at this stage we would not expect to see major breakthroughs because these take time. The point of this is simply to encourage people to keep going. Some may not have started yet so offer them some gentle encouragement too. Emphasize that doing a stronghold-buster is not a religious duty. If you miss a day, God is not cross with you! Just carry on from where you left off until you know that your thinking has changed. If there is someone who has a brief testimony of having done a stronghold-buster previously, that might be helpful.

WORSHIP

Lead a short time of worship.

OPENING PRAYER

Dear Heavenly Father,
Thank You that You have outrageously amazing plans for our lives but You give us complete free will as to whether to follow them or not. The decision is ours and whatever decision we make You will love us just the same. Father, in this session please show us the things that You have prepared for us to do that will make an eternal difference. Please fill us with the Holy Spirit and speak to us as we go through this final session.
In Jesus' name. Amen

DECLARATION

Our final declaration is on page 162 and helps people understand that the devil simply doesn't have the power to come in to our lives at will and disrupt them – unless, of course, we let him.

We declare that Jesus Christ came to destroy all of the works of the devil. The One who is in us is greater than the one who is in the world. As children of God, we declare that the devil must not interfere with what God has planned to do among us today. We declare the truth that the devil cannot prevent God's good plans for our lives.

STARTER FILM – DVD

This Starter Film raises the question, "Are you up for it?" and introduces the idea that God invites us to intertwine our stories with His bigger story and lead a life that not only makes an impact but leaves a legacy. He wants people who serve Him because they make a genuine choice to – not because they feel compelled to.

The first question is designed simply to get people sharing about interesting events they've been invited to in the past. Participants may suspect a trick question whereby they are meant to respond with "God's story" but reassure them that this is not the case!

KEY ONE – DVD

David affirms that as Christians, we are in Christ and that makes us ministers of reconciliation (2 Corinthians 5:17–20) and Jesus' ambassadors. We have everything we need to make our life stories count – but do we want to?

He then looks at 1 Corinthians 3:12–15 and invites everyone to build treasure in heaven that will last.

CHAT TIME ONE – PARTICIPANT'S GUIDE

In this Chat time we encourage participants to turn back to the first Chat time in the first session and look at what they said they wanted out of their life story at the beginning of the course. It will be interesting to see if and how this has changed over the course of the journey you have all taken together .

You will also discuss their identity as Jesus' ambassadors and the truth that Christ is IN them. If they can really connect to the reality that Jesus really does live in them it can be a very powerful revelation, which brings real transformation as the penny drops that what they are doing is offering themselves to God for Him to work through them. This is not about their strength but going on by God's Spirit.

KEY TWO – DVD

Jess looks in detail at Isaiah 61 and makes the point that this is the mandate God gives every believer. We are all called to share the good news – simply by being who we really are and fighting for justice and righteousness.

This should resonate with the millennial generation who feel strongly about equality and justice. We want people to understand that everyone can make a difference where they are right now by asking God what needs to change and how to bring that change.

Millennials tend to want to fit in with their peers and not risk upsetting people by stepping on their views. Jess encourages them to face their fears and be true to who they are by sharing her own vulnerability and that of the first disciples in stepping out. The message that comes out is that everyone feels fear but God is calling us to go for it – and we can!

CHAT TIME TWO – PARTICIPANT'S GUIDE

Before beginning this Chat, you might like to invite the group to stand and declare Isaiah 61:1–3 out loud together in the manner of the other declarations we have been making. It is printed on page 169. Get them to emphasize "me" – "The Lord has anointed me... He has sent me..." – and as they do so to recognize that this is their mandate from God.

This Chat gives participants time and space to explore their own fears about sharing their faith. They will likely find that they all have similar fears rooted in concern about offending people. It might be helpful to remind them of the discussion we had in Session 4 and have them recognize that these fears are rooted in a postmodern worldview. We need to remove the lens of postmodernism and look at reality the way God says it is.

Participants are also encouraged to explore the idea that they are the flesh and blood that God has chosen to work through if they allow Him to. Knowing that you are chosen but can still refuse to be used is an interesting and slightly disconcerting concept.

KEY THREE – DVD

In this final section Rob reiterates that we have a genuine choice. The last thing we want is for people to feel that we are telling them what they have to do. We want them to know that God invites them to respond but does not in any sense insist.

Rob takes them back to the story of the lost son in Luke 15:11–24 that we looked at in Session 1 and explores the likely impact of the father's love and grace on the younger son. Presumably he is doing much the same work that he hated before but now he does it willingly because he knows that he doesn't have to. The father will love him regardless. Some may ask if that means we can do whatever we like and it doesn't matter. The answer is that anyone who thinks like this has really not yet understood grace. When we truly take hold of God's love for us, we will choose to do what He wants us to because we love Him.

Rob then offers practical advice in working out how to follow God's call, making it clear that they can all serve God where they are at the moment. It's important that we don't inadvertently give the impression that work in a church or as a missionary overseas is somehow more important than work in the marketplace. All of us are ambassadors wherever God has put us and the job of the church is to prepare us for the works of service He has for us to do there (Ephesians 4:11–13).

Finally Rob looks at Mark 3:7–12 and notes the difference between the crowds who want simply to observe Jesus and the disciples who choose to follow Him.

To complete the course, Rob offers a prayer of commissioning which we would encourage everyone who wants to travel on as a disciple to engage with so that there is a sense of completion and being sent out.

REFLECT

It's our heart that each person will finish the course feeling that they have heard from God and know something of what He's calling them to do. Try to allow plenty of time for this final Reflect session.

We would suggest you pray beforehand and ask the Holy Spirit to speak to each person about their own situation. Then divide them into pairs or small groups to go through the questions.

CONCLUDING REMARKS

Point out the Going Deeper section in the Participant's Guide which encourages people to consider before God what it means to be an ambassador for Jesus in their own context.

Point out too the daily prayer and declaration on page 175 and the bedtime prayer on page 176 and recommend that people use them. Encourage them to keep going with those stronghold-busters and to continue to encourage each other to do them.

For those who want to do more work on their fear of speaking out for Jesus, Rob has put together a fantastic extra film called **"Overcoming Fear And Taking A Risk For Jesus"** that is accessible via the app. Young adults really struggle with fear and anxiety, and this will help them understand fear better and how to resolve it.

As they finish *disciple*, some of your group may be looking for opportunities to serve and would find it really helpful if you came with a list of suggestions of things that they could do in your church or locally. Try to come up with as many creative and inspiring opportunities as you can but ensure that there is no pressure put on people whatsoever to do them. Simply do as God does to us – offer an invitation.

You may like to read out the words on page 174 to round off *disciple*.

CLOSING PRAYER

Heavenly Father,

Thank You that You have called us to be fruitful disciples of Jesus. We have learnt so much as we have travelled this path together over these ten sessions. Please help us to stay on the right path, to use what we have learnt, to continue our stronghold-busters and follow You so that we can fulfil the plans You have for us, and use our life stories to do amazing things that make a real impact in Your kingdom. Thank You for Your truth and for the love and grace that You shower on us. Please anoint each and every one of us now and fill us with Your Holy Spirit. Send us out in joy and peace as ambassadors of Jesus so that everything we do will bring You glory.

In Jesus' name. Amen.

WHAT NEXT?

You might find it helpful to celebrate the end of *disciple* in some way. You could throw a bit of a party or enjoy a meal together. As part of that, you could invite participants to share briefly what difference the course has made to them.

You may also find that the group aren't keen to disband – that's a really good thing and we would encourage you to find a way to facilitate regular ongoing meetings even if you don't go yourself. Perhaps they can meet in a café or pub to share regularly what God is doing in their lives, or they may want to form a small group or an action group and work together on a project for God.

There are three further discipleship courses from Freedom In Christ Ministries that work well after *disciple*. If your church is running the main ***Freedom In Christ Course***, some of the group may want to attend that. They will receive the same messages over a longer period and in a different way and this can be a great reinforcement. ***The Grace Course*** is a six-week course that will help them look at guilt, shame, fear, and pride in a deeper way than we have been able to do on *disciple* and really take hold of the amazing truth of God's grace. Finally, ***Freed To Lead*** is a ten-week course for those in any kind of leadership position or who feel they may be leaders in the future. It's a leadership course like no other and focuses on leading from your identity in Christ and understanding and dealing with the realities of the spiritual world in organizations. Contact your local Freedom In Christ office for details.

One final thing: your group is still in the early stages of their stronghold-busters and probably approaching the time when they start to feel completely pointless. It's absolutely crucial to keep encouraging them. It can be as simple as dropping them a message every few days or as often as you feel necessary to ask them how it's going. If people have stopped, remember, that's no big deal. Just encourage them to start again where they left off.